EXCEPTIONALITY, *13*(1), 1–2
Copyright © 2005, Lawrence Erlbaum Associates, Inc.

I0128972

PREFACE

Autism and Applied Behavior Analysis

Individuals in the field of education have heard the figures of dramatic increases in the prevalence of autism. Undoubtedly, they have known teachers and parents who are seeking strategies to educate their children with unique behavioral, social, and communication characteristics. Further, they have most likely been exposed to information available on the Internet, with many sites claiming to have the panacea for whatever ails. Where can educators and parents turn to secure current and accurate information about issues related to autism?

Applied behavior analysis (ABA) offers an empirical basis for diagnosis, assessment, and instruction for individuals with autism. ABA is the only therapy or treatment endorsed by the United States Surgeon General (2000) and is considered by many to be the "standard approach" for individuals with autism (see the article in this issue by Shook & Neisworth). ABA, in its simplest terms, is science used to improve behavior of importance (Cooper, Heron, & Heward, 1987). In ABA, science is taken out of the carefully controlled laboratory and put to use in the "real world" where it is used in places like classrooms, living rooms, and the community. With its tenets of science, ABA has seven dimensions (Baer, Wolf, & Risley, 1968): (a) applied (the outcome has practical significance), (b) behavioral (behavior itself is of interest), (c) analytical (functional relationships can be established), (d) technological (procedures are described so that studies can be replicated), (e) conceptually systematic (derived from basic theoretical principles), (f) effective (there are socially important outcomes), and (g) generalized (changes are evident over time and settings).

In this issue of *Exceptionality,* we present articles from a number of professionals involved in research and training related to autism and ABA. In the first article, Shook and Neisworth outline the need for behavior analysts who are well trained. They discuss the creation of a national credentialing board (Behavior Analyst Certification Board). Further, Shook and Neisworth detail several university programs that are providing much needed training.

As a group, behavior analysts began to formally organize and publish research beginning in the early 1960s. Examination of the past can help characterize our present and future as a field. Wolery, Barton, and Hine examine changes in the field by reviewing articles appearing in *Journal of Applied Behavior Analysis,* a premiere outlet for applied research. The authors review research related to persons with autism over the last three decades. Wolery et al. find significant shifts in what issues are researched and how treatment is conducted. The authors offer an opportunity to examine the "evolution" of ABA and autism as well as the direction of research.

In the third article, Iwata and Worsdell discuss the recommended practice of functional analysis. A cornerstone of ABA, functional analysis is described, methods for assessing determinants of problem behavior are detailed, and recommended practices are given.

Kubina and Wolfe address an aspect of performance criterion that may be especially important for individuals with autism—fluency. The authors make the case that previous research has looked only at mastery to a certain criterion. Fluent, or accurate and automatic, responses are an important performance criterion and standard. Kubina and Wolfe outline a number of learning outcomes associated with behavioral fluency, including retention, endurance, and application. Although an emerging technology, fluency measures offer an important performance standard for learners with autism.

Using single-subject design, Neidert, Iwata, and Dozier provide an application of functional analysis with two children having autism. The authors provide an excellent illustration of how assessment and instruction relate. In this study, functional analyses indicated that the behaviors were maintained by both positive and negative reinforcement. Using principles of ABA, Neidert et al. detail a successful intervention.

In the final article of this special issue, Tucci, Hursh, Laitinen, and Lambe describe the Competent Learner Model (CLM). The CLM provides a comprehensive and useful model for providing ABA principles systemwide. In place in multiple sites in California, there is compelling evidence of successful student outcomes as well as parent and staff satisfaction. The model provides an integrated method for the assessment and delivery of instruction and incorporates best practice strategies such as individual and group instruction. Tucci et al. provide a systemic model that brings it all together and offers, we think, a fitting way to close the issue.

We hope you enjoy the articles assembled for this issue of *Exceptionality*. Working with individuals with autism presents numerous challenges; however, as the authors in the issue can attest, there are exciting advances to be made in research and practice. Using the theoretical basis of ABA we can continue to examine the evolution of the field of autism.

REFERENCES

Baer, D. M., Wolf, M. M., & Risley, T. (1968). Current dimensions of applied behavior analysis. *Journal of Applied Behavior Analysis, 1,* 91–97.

Cooper, J. O., Heron, T. E., & Heward, W. E. (1987). *Applied behavior analysis.* Columbus, OH: Merrill.

United States Surgeon General. (2000). *Report of the United States Surgeon General: Chap. 3. Children and mental health.* Retrieved February 14, 2001, from http://www.surgeongeneral.gov/library/mentalhealth/chapter3/sec6.html#autism

Pamela Wolfe and John T. Neisworth
Guest Editors

EXCEPTIONALITY, *13*(1), 3–10
Copyright © 2005, Lawrence Erlbaum Associates, Inc.

ARTICLES

Ensuring Appropriate Qualifications for Applied Behavior Analyst Professionals: The Behavior Analyst Certification Board

Gerald L. Shook
Behavior Analyst Certification Board
Tallahassee, Florida

John T. Neisworth
Professor Emeritus
Pennsylvania State University

The escalating numbers of people identified with autism and other pervasive developmental disorders has resulted in a corresponding increase in the demand for behavior specialists who can direct and conduct applied behavior analytic interventions. There are, however, severe shortages in professionals who can deliver quality services. In this article we describe the credentialing process and requirements of the Behavior Analyst Certification Board® (BACB®). University training is now available in numerous states through BACB-approved course sequences. The growth of the BACB, an illustration of a university-approved program, and implications for treatment programs are discussed.

Applied behavior analysis is built on the solid empirical foundation of experimental research (e.g., *Journal of the Experimental Analysis of Behavior,* 1958–present) and applied research (e.g., *Journal of Applied Behavior Analysis,* 1968–present). It has become the evidence-based treatment of choice for those with autism (Howard, Sparkman, Cohen, Green, & Stanislaw, 2005), and it is the only approach with scientifically documented effectiveness available for children with autism (New York State Department of Health, Early Intervention Program, 1999; United States Surgeon General, 2000). In addition, much of the general public considers applied behavior analysis to be the "standard approach" in instruction and treatment for people with autism, as is evidenced in popular publications addressing the subject (Cowley, 2000).

Requests for reprints should be sent to Gerald L. Shook, Behavior Analyst Certification Board, 1705 Metropolitan Boulevard, Suite 102, Tallahassee, FL 32308. E-mail: shook@bacb.com

This preeminence of applied behavior analysis as the instruction and treatment method of choice with people with autism has led to a considerable increase in consumer demand for behavior analyst professionals and services. Because of this demand, and the subsequent increased availability of funding for behavior analytic services for children with autism, many unqualified individuals, who do not have the necessary training or experience, have claimed to be behavior analysts and have provided questionable services for these children. This unfortunate development is a major concern to all manner of consumers of behavior analytic services, including parents, teachers, school administrators, governmental departments of education, and citizens concerned with good education and the prudent use of taxpayer funds. Consumers simply could not easily identify qualified behavior analyst professionals, and there was no good mechanism in place to protect consumers from unqualified behavior analysts.

Credentialing of behavior analytic professionals has been developed, in large part, to protect the public and help individuals identify qualified behavior analysts, and it is an integral part of ensuring the delivery of quality behavior analysis services (Johnston & Shook, 1993; Moore & Shook, 2001; Shook & Favell, 1996; Shook & Van Houten, 1993).

PROFESSIONAL CREDENTIALS

The most common way of identifying qualified professionals in most fields is through their professional credential; for example, teachers are certified, and attorneys are licensed. Because most of these established professional credentials are based on accepted national credentialing standards (American Educational Research Association, American Psychological Association, and National Council on Measurement in Education, 1999; National Organization for Competency Assurance, 2002; United States Equal Employment Opportunity Commission, 1978), the credential gives consumers some assurance that the professionals who possess them have met at least specified minimum professional standards.

Until recently, behavior analyst professionals and consumers have not had access to a professional credential. Some other professionals (e.g., psychologists with graduate degrees) are allowed by law to practice behavior analysis; however, their credentials do not ensure that they have met minimum standards of training, professional experience, and knowledge in behavior analysis. The credentialing examinations of other professions contain little or no behavior analytic content, and individuals who pass these examinations could miss all behavior analysis questions but become credentialed in those professions. In addition, the eligibility requirements to take those examinations do not include academic training or professional experience specifically in behavior analysis, and continuing education in behavior analysis is not required to maintain the credential. Undoubtedly, there are qualified behavior analyst professionals who are credentialed in other professions, but that credential does not specify or assure behavior analytic preparation and knowledge.

BEHAVIOR ANALYST CERTIFICATION

The state of Florida identified the need to credential behavior analysts and began the process in the mid-1980s (Starin, Hemingway, & Hartsfield, 1993). Florida developed its behavior analyst certification examinations in keeping with professional standards and in compliance with relevant case law pertaining to professional credentialing. Certification programs using the Florida model and examinations were soon developed in Oklahoma, Texas, California, Pennsylvania, and New York. However, as more states and the practitioners within them identified the need for a certification processes, it became apparent that a national certification board for behavior analyst practitioners was needed. The Behavior Analyst Certification Board® (BACB®) was formed in 1998 in response to this need. Subsequently, all state-based certification programs have closed and turned all of the responsibility for certification over to the BACB.

The BACB offers behavior analyst certification at two levels: Board Certified Behavior Analyst™ (BCBA®) and Board Certified Associate Behavior Analyst™ (BCABA®). Each of these certification levels has specific degree, coursework, and experience requirements that applicants must meet to be eligible to take the BCBA or BCABA written examination. The following requirements will go into effect following the 2005 spring examinations application deadlines.

BCBA applicants must have at least a master's degree, specific graduate coursework in behavior analysis, and supervised professional experience in the practice of behavior analysis. The master's degree may be in any area of study. The coursework requirement consists of 225 classroom hours of behavior analytic content, which is equivalent to 15 semester credit hours, or five 3-hr graduate-level courses. The coursework must include content in areas such as basic principles of behavior, application of these basic principles, behavioral assessment, single-subject design, and ethics. Courses prepared and offered by universities can be submitted to the BACB for approval to assure that students taking the courses will meet course requirements set by that board. For a detailed listing of the required content areas and the number of classroom hours of instruction required for each, see Table 1. The supervised professional experience requirement consists of 9 months of experience wherein the applicant is engaged in behavior analytic activities for at least 20 hr per week. The supervisor must meet with the applicant on a prespecified schedule and provide feedback regarding performance. A less intensive mentoring arrangement that does not require face-to-face interaction is also available for individuals who do not have ready access to a supervisor. Because the mentored experience is less intensive, applicants must have 18 months of this type of experience to qualify to take the examination.

BCABA applicants must have at least a bachelors' degree, specific undergraduate or graduate coursework in behavior analysis, and supervised professional experience in the practice of behavior analysis. The bachelor's degree may be in any area of study. The coursework requirement consists of 125 classroom hours of behavior analytic content, which is equivalent to 9 semester credit hours, or three 3-hr courses. The coursework must include content in areas such as basic principles of behavior, application of these basic principles, behavioral assessment, single-subject design, and ethics. For a detailed listing of the required content areas for BCABA and the number of classroom hours of instruction required for each, see Table 1. Applicants also must have at least 4½ months of supervised experience, or 9 months of mentored experience, in an appropriate applied setting.

Applicants who have met the eligibility requirements, at either the BCBA or BCABA level, must take and pass a written examination to become certified at their chosen level. The examinations have been professionally developed and maintained since the mid-1980s, initially by the state of Florida and more recently by the BACB.

TABLE 1
Contact Hour Requirement Per Content Area

	Contact Hours	
Content Area	BCBA	BCABA
1. Ethical considerations	15	10
2. Definition and characteristics and 3. Principles, processes, and concepts	45	40
4. Behavioral assessment and 8. Selecting intervention outcomes and strategies	35	25
5. Experimental evaluation of interventions	20	20[a]
6. Measurement of behavior and 7. Displaying and interpreting behavioral data	20	
9. Behavior change procedures and 10. Systems support	45	40
11. Discretionary[b]	45	0
Totals	225	135

Note. BCBA = Board Certified Behavior Analyst; BCABA = Board Certified Associate Behavior Analyst.

[a]For BCABA, 20 hr is the total for Content Areas 5, 6, and 7 (not just for Content Areas 6 and 7 as for BCBA). [b]May be used within any one or more of the 10 content areas or for any applications of behavior analysis. For example, this could be used for behavior analytic applications in topic areas such as autism, organizational behavior management, behavioral pharmacology, and so on, as long as the coursework contact hours that are listed are behavior analysis applications (not including behavior therapy).

Content for the examination was developed through a series of three systematic Job Analyses that were conducted every 5 to 8 years in accordance with the accepted professional standards and applicable case law in the area of credentialing (Shook, Johnston, & Mellichamp, 2004). These examinations are the foundation of the BACB certification program and, as are all aspects of the program, are developed to be consistent with the highest professional standards (Shook, 2005).

As is the case for most other professionals, BCBAs and BCABAs must obtain specific continuing education units to maintain their certifications. This process is designed to help ensure that BACB certificants continue to be current in new developments in the practice of applied behavior analysis. These individuals must renew their certification annually and provide documentation of earning the appropriate number of continuing education units at the close of their 3-year recertification cycle.

UNIVERSITY TRAINING

University training is an integral component of the certification process when preparing individuals to instruct children with autism (Shook, Rosales, & Glenn, 2002). Although the BACB will accept appropriate coursework from any qualified university, most applicants now obtain their training from universities with BACB-approved course sequences. The BACB approves course sequences for preparation at both the BCBA and BCABA levels. Universities with BACB-approved course sequences can ensure that students who successfully complete the sequence will meet the coursework requirements at the approved level, and the university may advertise this approval status. Students completing the sequence will be assured of meeting the coursework requirement and will not have to provide as much coursework documentation during the application process.

Universities may choose to integrate training in behavioral applications in instructing children with autism into the BACB-approved course sequence. This may be accomplished by various means, including using examples relating to autism instruction to meet the application of basic principles content requirement or by having the discretionary course in BCBA training relate to behavior analysis in autism.

As an illustration, the Penn State University course sequence in applied behavior analysis consists of four courses (15 semester-credits) delivered through a continuing education distance-type format. The first three courses are 4 semester-credits each and cover the BACB-specified content areas but not the 45 hr of discretionary content. These 45 hr (3 semester-credits) are provided through an Extended Applications course offered on the Penn State campus. Students who cannot or choose not to attend the on-campus course but need the additional academic credit to qualify for certification examination may take appropriate courses at a local university or through a BACB-approved online course. Alternatively, students needing the additional academic credit and who wish to focus on autism-related applications may choose to enroll in Autism and Applied Behavior Analysis, a 3-credit specialty course in the Penn State Autism Continuing Education program. On-campus, in-residence students may elect as part of their graduate programs any of the courses just mentioned. Since 1998, 586 persons have successfully completed the Penn State applied behavior analysis course sequence, including students from 23 states as well as from Canada, Jamaica, and Sweden. The Penn State enrollments have shown growth parallel to the national increases.

GROWTH OF THE BACB

Since the inception of the BACB, the number of certificants credentialed by the BACB has grown substantially (see Figure 1). Although the current number of certificants is not adequate to meet the national or international need for qualified behavior analysts, the numbers have grown impressively for such a young program, with nearly 4,000 certificants currently in 48 states and 20 countries.

Of course, growth of the certificant base is closely tied to the number of universities with BACB-approved course sequences, and this number also has grown impressively over the past few years (see Figure 2).

In only 4 years, 72 universities have received BACB approval of one or more of their course sequences. Of the 94 approved sequences, 60 are graduate programs approved at the BCBA level, and 34 are approved at the BCABA level. Nine of the sequences are distance learning, and 10 of the sequences are offered in universities outside the United States.

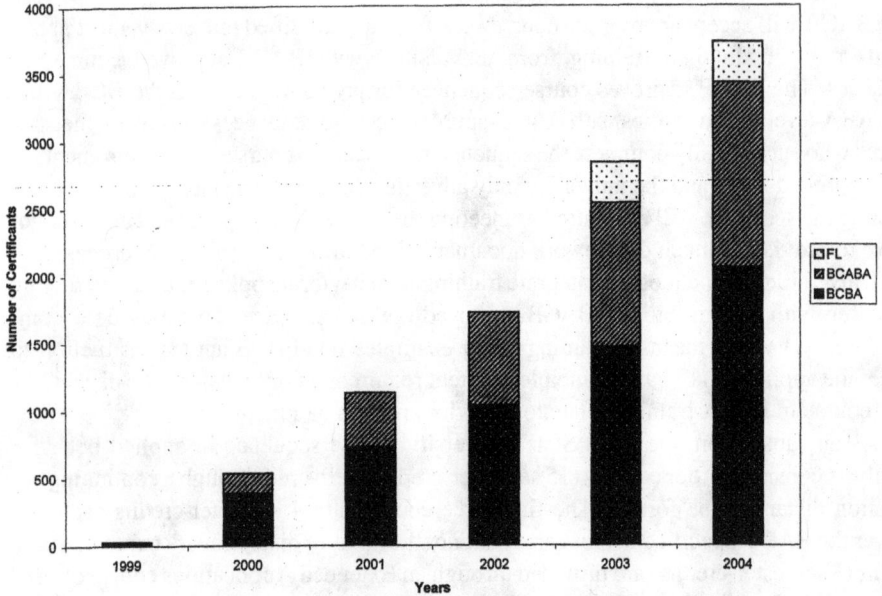

FIGURE 1   Number of certificants credentialed by the Behavior Analyst Certification Board. FL = individuals retaining Florida certificates; BCABA = Board Certified Associate Behavior Analyst; BCBA = Board Certified Behavior Analyst.

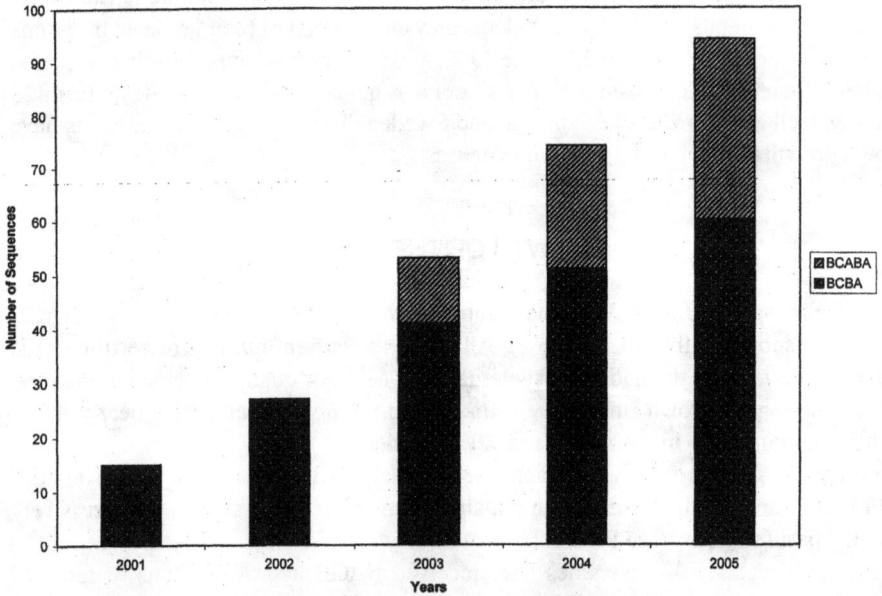

FIGURE 2   Number of course sequences approved by the Behavior Analyst Certification Board. BCABA = Board Certified Associate Behavior Analyst; BCBA = Board Certified Behavior Analyst.

IMPLICATIONS FOR CHILDREN WITH AUTISM

The BACB credentialing process provides confidence for consumers that the certificant has met the established requirements for certification and therefore has at least entry-level competence in the application of behavior analysis. However, this credential alone is not all that is required of a practitioner who will instruct children with autism. For consumers, certification as a BCBA or BCABA may be viewed as a necessary but not alone sufficient indicator of competence for behavior analyst professionals who will provide instruction for these individuals.

Consumers should look carefully at other aspects of the professional's credentials and ask some important questions such as the following:

- Was the individual's university training obtained in a BACB-approved course sequence that emphasized training in behavior analytic applications with children with autism?
- Did the individual obtain his or her experience under a supervisor who was well trained and experienced in autism?
- What was the nature and intensity of the supervision?
- Did the setting in which the person obtained professional experience offer the opportunity to work with children with autism in an appropriate manner?
- What recommendations can the individual provide from consumers and professionals with whom he or she has worked?

Of course, a specialty certification in the applications of applied behavior analysis in individuals with autism, in addition to an existing BACB credential and the precautions just outlined, could provide the best assurance to consumers that professionals are qualified in this area. The BACB is aware of this need and may consider offering a specialty certificate when considerable development resources required to complete the involved task have been identified.

CONCLUSIONS

Applied behavior analysis is the sole evidence-based treatment for individuals who have autism and has become the preferred approach. In addition, the utility of applied behavior analysis is evident in assessing behavior, identifying accessible variables for designing instruction, and scientifically evaluating outcomes. Methods such as functional behavior assessment, direct instruction, discrete trial training, analysis and teaching of verbal behavior, precision teaching, fluency training, contingency management and contracting, early intensive behavioral intervention, and numerous other instructional approaches are applications of applied behavior analysis.

The BACB identifies important competencies for behavior analysts, approves relevant university behavior analytic coursework, requires specific behavior analytic experience and coursework from applicants, provides certification examinations in applied behavior analysis built to professional standards, and requires continuing education to maintain certificants' competence in behavior analysis. The expert use of applied behavior analysis provides evidenced-based cost-effective services that result in measurable outcomes; the BACB is the major professional organization helping to ensure that qualified professionals provide these services.

Additional information can be found on the BACB's Web site: http://www.BACB.com.

ACKNOWLEDGMENTS

The trademarks "Behavior Analyst Certification Board, Inc.," "BACB," "Board Certified Behavior Analyst," "BCBA," "Board Certified Associate Behavior Analyst," and "BCABA" are owned by the Behavior Analyst Certification Board. All rights reserved.

REFERENCES

American Educational Research Association, American Psychological Association, and National Council on Measurement in Education. (1999). *Standards for educational and psychological testing*. Washington, DC: American Psychological Association.

Cowley, G. (2000, July 31). Understanding autism. *Newsweek*, pp. 46–54.

Howard, J., Sparkman, C., Cohen, H., Green, G., & Stanislaw, H. (2005). A comparison of intensive behavior analytic and eclectic treatments for young children with autism. *Research in Developmental Disabilities, 26*, 359–383.

Johnston, J. M., & Shook, G. L. (1993). A model for the statewide delivery of programming services. *Mental Retardation, 31*, 127–139.

Moore, J., & Shook, G. L. (2001). Certification, accreditation and quality control in behavior analysis. *The Behavior Analyst, 24*, 45–55.

National Organization for Competency Assurance. (2002). *National Commission for Certifying Agencies standards for accreditation of national certification programs*. Washington, DC: Author.

New York State Department of Health, Early Intervention Program. (1999). *Clinical practice guideline: Report of the recommendations: Autism/PDD, assessment and intervention for young children*. Albany, NY: Author.

Shook, G. L. (2005). An examination of the integrity and future of Behavior Analyst Certification Board credentials. *Behavior Modification, 29*, 562–574.

Shook, G. L., & Favell, J. E. (1996). Identifying qualified professionals in behavior analysis. In C. Maurice, G. Green, & S. C. Luce (Eds.), *Behavioral intervention for young children with autism: A manual for parents and professionals* (pp. 221–229). Austin, TX: Pro-Ed.

Shook, G. L., Johnston, J. M., & Mellichamp, F. (2004). Determining essential content for applied behavior analyst practitioners. *The Behavior Analyst, 27*, 67–94.

Shook, G. L., Rosales, S. A., & Glenn, S. (2002). Certification and training of behavior analyst professionals. *Behavior Modification, 26*, 27–48.

Shook, G. L., & Van Houten, R. (1993). Ensuring the competence of behavior analysts. In R. Van Houten & S. Axelrod (Eds.), *Behavior analysis and treatment* (pp. 171–181). New York: Plenum.

Starin, S., Hemingway, M., & Hartsfield, F. (1993). Credentialing behavior analysts and the Florida behavior analysis certification program. *The Behavior Analyst, 16*, 153–166.

United States Equal Employment Opportunity Commission. (1978). *United States Equal Employment Opportunity Commission guidelines on employment testing procedures*. Washington, DC: Author.

United States Surgeon General. (2000). *Report of the United States Surgeon General: Chap. 3. Children and mental health*. Retrieved February 14, 2001, from http://www.surgeongeneral.gov/library/mentalhealth/chapter3/sec6.html#autism

EXCEPTIONALITY, *13*(1), 11–23

Evolution of Applied Behavior Analysis in the Treatment of Individuals With Autism

Mark Wolery, Erin E. Barton, and Jeffrey F. Hine

Department of Special Education
Peabody College, Vanderbilt University

Two issues of each volume of the *Journal of Applied Behavior Analysis* were reviewed to identify research reports focusing on individuals with autism. The identified articles were analyzed to describe the ages of individuals with autism, the settings in which the research occurred, the nature of the behaviors targeted for intervention, and the independent variables used. The data are analyzed in terms of shifts over time. These data were used to present a description of the changes in applied behavior analysis work related to individuals with autism.

Autism is a developmental disability and was identified more than 60 years ago by Leo Kanner (1943). It is characterized as a spectrum of disorders in which pronounced impairments are present in social and language–communication domains accompanied by ritualistic and challenging behaviors (National Research Council, 2001). Autism spectrum disorders are diagnosed in the early childhood period, often as early as 24 months and usually by 42 months.

Over the years, a variety of intervention approaches with varying levels of research support have been recommended and used in the treatment of the condition (Handleman & Harris, 2000); one of those approaches is applied behavior analysis (ABA). ABA, as used in this article, does not refer to a specific intervention program, as is often the case in colloquial descriptions of treatment programs (Schwartz, Billingsley, & Wolery, 1999); rather, it refers to investigations based in the field of ABA.

Baer, Wolf, and Risley (1968) described the dimensions of ABA in the inaugural issue of the *Journal of Applied Behavior Analysis* (*JABA*). They proposed ABA had seven dimensions. First, it was *applied* because the studies focused on behaviors and issues of importance to society. Second, ABA was *behavioral,* meaning it used direct measures of participants' behaviors, allowing low levels of inference about the phenomenon being studied. Third, ABA was *analytical,* meaning investigators used experimental designs and procedures, allowing them to document their experimental manipulations were re-

Requests for reprints should be sent to Mark Wolery, Department of Special Education, Peabody College, Box 328, Vanderbilt University, Nashville, TN 37203–5721. E-mail: mark.wolery@vanderbilt.edu

lated functionally to the behaviors being measured. Fourth, ABA was *technological,* meaning the experimental operations and variables were defined operationally and at replicable levels. Fifth, ABA was *conceptually systematic,* meaning the experimental manipulations and the resulting findings were put in the context of a coherent framework for understanding and explaining human behavior. Sixth, ABA was *effective,* meaning it produced changes in participants' behavior large enough to be useful to them. Finally, ABA involved studies with *generality,* meaning a durable effect occurred on the participants' life outside of the experimental context.

The purpose of this article is to describe the evolution of ABA as described by Baer et al. (1968) in the treatment of individuals with autism. The following research questions were asked: (a) Who are the participants involved in the autism treatment research? (b) What were the ages of individuals with autism studied in this research? (c) Where (what settings) did the studies occur? (d) What primary dependent variables were measured? and (e) What interventions have been evaluated in that research? Of interest for this article are the shifts that have occurred over the time period since the dimensions of ABA were first identified and described.

METHOD

Sample

ABA studies evaluating interventions for treating individuals with autism are published in a wide variety of periodicals. For this review, investigations were restricted to those published in *JABA.* The rationale for restricting the review to *JABA* was to increase the likelihood that the reviewed studies were consistent with the dimensions of ABA as described by Baer et al. (1968). Each article in two issues of each volume of *JABA* from Volume 1 (1968) to Volume 36 (2003) was screened. The two issues for each volume were selected randomly using a random number table.

Procedures

Three individuals reviewed the selected issues of *JABA* using the following steps: For each full article (brief reports were excluded) in the selected issues, the reviewer initially examined the article's participant section. An article was selected for review if at least one participant was diagnosed as having autism, pervasive developmental disorders not otherwise specified, Asperger's disorder, childhood disintegrative disorder, Rett syndrome, or childhood schizophrenia (used in the early 1970s), or if at least one participant was described as autistic-like. Hereafter, the participants are referred to as *participants with autism.* If the participants were adults and described as having schizophrenia, the article was not included. These various diagnostic groups were included to encompass the dates of publication of reviewed articles. In addition, an article was included if the participants were teachers or other professionals who worked with individuals who had autism (e.g., training teachers to use a particular strategy with individuals with autism). Finally, an article was included if the participants were family members (e.g., parents or siblings) of individuals with autism.

The following information was recorded for each article: (a) number of participants, (b) number of participants with autism, (c) whether other participants (professionals and family members) were the participants, (d) age of participants with autism, (e) setting in which the study occurred, (f) intervention evaluated in the study, (g) description of the primary dependent measures, and (h) whether a functional analysis of the behavior being studied was described. The settings were further subdivided into the following categories: home, clinic, research lab, hospital (inpatient), school (integrated class, segregated class, therapy room, playground, and could not tell), and other. The settings were further coded as the primary setting of data collection or as a generalization setting. The relevant portions of the method section and the purpose statement at the end of the introduction were reviewed. The data were entered on a specifically developed data sheet and then entered into a database program for analysis. To minimize bias in the review of the volumes across time, each reviewer was assigned to every third volume. The reviewers also counted the total number of full articles in each issue.

RESULTS

In the two selected issues of each of the 36 volumes of *JABA* from 1968 to 2003, 605 articles were screened. Of these, 99 (16.4%) of the articles met the criteria as having participants with autism. These data were reviewed to determine if changes occurred across time. The 36 volumes of *JABA* were divided in three equal time periods (Volumes 1–12, 13–24, and 25–36). The number and percentage of articles with participants who had autism across the three time periods were 23 articles (9.7% of the published articles), 29 articles (16.3%), and 47 articles (24.7%), respectively. This appears to indicate an increase in the proportion of articles published in *JABA* that include participants with autism.

Number of Participants With Autism

There were 464 participants involved in the 99 selected articles, and 300 (64.7%) were individuals with autism. The number and proportion of participants with autism for each of the three time periods of the journal in the selected articles were 79 (76%), 112 (67.5%), and 109 (56.2%), respectively. Of the 99 articles with participants who had autism, 12 (12.1%) had only 1 participant in the study. A majority (7, or 58.3%) of these articles were published in the first 12 volumes, 1 (8.3%) was published in Volumes 13 to 24, and 4 (33.3%) were published in Volumes 25 to 36. A majority (55, or 55.5%) of the articles had participants with autism only. Across the three time periods, the proportion of articles including participants with autism only declined: 69.6%, 62.1%, and 44.7%, respectively. Thus, although the percentage of articles in *JABA* with participants who had autism increased over time, the percentage of articles containing only participants with autism and the percentage of participants with autism decreased.

Other Participants

The selected articles also were analyzed to determine if other participants in the studies were family members (parents and siblings) of the participants with autism, teachers or other professionals, and peers. The number and percentage of such articles are shown in Table 1. None of the selected articles included siblings of the participants with autism as participants, 5 articles included parents, and 5 articles included teachers or other professionals. Peers, often classmates, of the individual with autism were included in 10 articles, all of which were published in the last 24 volumes of the journal. Thus, a large majority (80.8%) of the selected articles did not include participants other than individuals with autism or other disabilities.

Age of Participants With Autism

The ages of the participants with autism in the 99 articles were recorded and analyzed. One article did not report the ages of participants, and 11 articles reported an age range. For the remaining articles, the ages of each participant was reported. The mean age was 11.1 years, with a range of 2 to 45 years. Across the three time periods of *JABA,* the means and ranges were 9.0 years (3–20), 8.9 (2–22), and 11.4 (3–45), respectively. The ages of participants were divided into five age categories (0–5, 6–10, 11–15, 16–20, and 21 or older). The number and percentage of participants at each age range for the three time periods and across all time periods are shown in Table 2. The data in Table 2 indicate that a majority of the individuals with autism in the reviewed articles were 6 to 10 years of age. The percentage of participants with autism 5 years of age or younger appears to be increasing over time, although it only accounts for 18.7% of the participants with autism. Similarly, the percentage of older participants with autism (ages 16–20 and older than 21 years) is increasing but constitutes a relatively small number of participants. Nine of 11 articles included age ranges (rather than specific ages) that spanned the categories shown in Table 2. Of these, four (with 21 participants) spanned the under 5 and the

TABLE 1
Number and Percentage of Articles by Type of Participants Related
to the Participants With Autism Across Time Periods

Type of Participant	Volumes 1–12[a] No. of Articles	%	Volumes 13–24[b] No. of Articles	%	Volumes 25–36[c] No. of Articles	%	All Volumes[d] No. of Articles	%
Parents of participant with autism	3	13.0	1	3.5	1	2.1	5	5.1
Siblings of participant with autism	0	—	0	—	0	—	0	—
Teacher or other professional	2	8.7	1	3.5	2	4.2	5	5.1
Peers of individual with autism	0	0.0	6	20.7	4	8.5	10	10.1

[a]$n = 23$. [b]$n = 29$. [c]$n = 47$. [d]$n = 99$.

TABLE 2
Number and Percentage of Participants With Autism by Age

Age Range	Volumes 1–12[a]		Volumes 13–24[b]		Volumes 25–36[c]		All Volumes[d]	
	No. of Participants	%	No. of Participants	%	No. of Participants	%	No. of Participants	%
≤5 years	6	10.2	18	22.5	18	20.9	42	18.7
6–10 years	37	62.7	42	52.5	34	39.5	113	50.2
11–15 years	15	25.4	12	15.0	19	22.1	46	20.4
16–20 years	1	1.7	6	7.5	8	9.3	15	6.7
≥21 years	0	0.0	2	2.5	7	8.1	9	4.0

[a]$n = 59$. [b]$n = 80$. [c]$n = 86$. [d]$n = 225$.

6-to-10 age ranges; two (with 11 participants) spanned the 6-to-10 and 11-to-15 age ranges; two (with 19 participants) spanned the under 5, 6-to-10, and 11-to-15 age ranges; and one (with 4 participants) spanned the 11-to-15 and 16-to-20 age ranges.

Study Settings

The articles were analyzed to identify the primary and generalization settings used in the selected studies. Primary setting was defined as the location in which the independent variable was implemented and the dependent measure was collected. One article did not identify the primary setting. For two articles, two primary settings were used: In one article, the home and clinic were primary settings; in the second, an inclusive class and lunchroom were used. All remaining articles had one primary setting. The number and percentage of articles using different types of primary settings are reported in Table 3. The most frequently used primary setting was schools (51.5%), followed by hospitals or other residential facilities (21.2%), research labs (12.1%), and clinics (11.1%). Over time (i.e., Volumes 1–12, 13–24, 25–36), the percentage of articles in which schools and research labs were used decreased slightly, whereas the percentage of residential facilities and clinics increased. Homes and the community were not used as a primary setting until the third time period. Within schools, the percentage of articles using integrated classrooms (those including students without disabilities) increased across the three time periods, whereas separate classes (those including only students with disabilities) decreased, as did the use of therapy rooms.

Data also were collected on the use of generalization settings; data were not collected on generalization across materials, persons, or time. Generalization across settings occurred in 21 (21.2%) of the articles—3 (13%) of the articles in Volumes 1 to 12, 8 (27.6%) in Volumes 13 to 24, and 10 (21.3%) in Volumes 25 to 36. In Volumes 1 to 12, the home was used twice and a separate classroom was used once. In Volumes 13 to 24, the home was used twice (once from a clinic and once from a therapy room at school), a separate classroom was used twice (once from a therapy room and once from another part of the separate classroom), the playground was used in four articles (twice from a therapy room, once from a clinic, and once from a separate classroom),

TABLE 3
Number and Percentage of Articles by Primary Setting

Type of Setting	Volumes 1–12[a] No. of Articles	%	Volumes 13–24[b] No. of Articles	%	Volumes 25–36[c] No. of Articles	%	All Volumes[d] No. of Articles	%
Home	0	—	0	—	3[e]	6.4	3[e]	3.0
Clinic	2	8.7	3	10.4	6[e]	12.8	11[e]	11.1
Research lab	5	21.7	3	10.4	4	8.5	12	12.1
Hospital (residential facility)	2	8.7	7	24.1	12	25.5	21	21.2
School	13	56.5	16	55.2	22	46.8	51	51.5
Inclusive class	1	7.9	2	12.5	9	40.9	12	23.5
Separate class	7	53.9	7	43.8	8	36.4	22	43.1
Therapy room	5	38.5	6	37.5	4	18.2	15	29.4
Playground	0	—	1	6.3	0	—	1	2.0
Other	0	—	0	—	1[f]	4.6	1[f]	2.0
Could not tell	0	—	0	—	1[g]	4.6	1[g]	2.0
Other (community)	0	—	0	—	1[h]	2.1	1[h]	1.0
Could not tell	1	4.3	0	—	0	—	1	1.0

[a]$n = 23$. [b]$n = 29$. [c]$n = 47$. [d]$n = 99$. [e]Data collected at a clinic and at home. [f]Data collected at school in an integrated class and in the lunchroom. [g]Data collected at school but could not determine the location within the school. [h]Data collected in the community.

and a bathroom in school was used once from a separate class. In Volumes 25 to 36, the home was used three times (twice from a research laboratory and once from a clinic), a school (unspecified location) was used once from a residential facility, integrated classes were used three times (once each from an integrated class, separate class, and therapy room), playgrounds were used twice (once each from a separate classroom and therapy room at school), and community sites were used three times. None of the articles in Volumes 1 to 12 used multiple generalization settings, but two did for Volumes 13 to 24, and three did for Volumes 25 to 36. Thus, use of generalization settings occurs more frequently in more recent volumes; the settings in which generalization are measured are quite varied.

Purpose and Focus of Research

Research reports in *JABA* are almost exclusively experimental studies evaluating a specific environmental manipulation, and the reviewed articles represented this tradition. The articles were analyzed to determine whether the focus of the research was to (a) increase (accelerate) participants' performance, (b) decrease (decelerate) performance, or (c) both accelerate and decelerate performance. The number and percentage of articles by these three categories across the three time periods of publication are shown in Table 4. As shown, the largest percentage of articles in the first time period focused on both accelerating and decelerating participants' performance; during the remaining two times periods, a majority of the articles focused only on accelerating participants' behavior. The percentage of articles focusing only on decelerating participants' behav-

TABLE 4
Number and Percentage of Articles by Focus on Participants' Behavior

Purpose	Volumes 1–12[a]		Volumes 13–24[b]		Volumes 25–36[c]		All Volumes[d]	
	No. of Articles	%	No. of Articles	%	No. of Articles	%	No. of Articles	%
Accelerate (increase) participants' behavior	7	30.4	18	62.1	24	51.1	49	49.5
Decelerate (decrease) participants' behavior	6	26.1	3	10.4	13	27.7	22	22.2
Accelerate some behaviors and decelerate other behaviors	10	43.5	8	27.6	10	21.3	28	28.3

[a]$n = 23$. [b]$n = 29$. [c]$n = 47$. [d]$n = 99$.

ior dipped during the middle time period but was relatively similar in the first and third time periods.

The dependent measures of the articles were analyzed to describe more precisely the types of behaviors being addressed. These data are shown in Table 5. For acceleration targets (i.e., measuring an increase in behavior either with or without also measuring a decrease in another behavior), language/communication and social skills constituted a majority of the articles (55.5%), with language/communication skills receiving more attention than social skills. Nearly one third of the articles included a measure of language/communication skills, and this was relatively stable across the three time periods. Articles measuring social behavior constituted slightly more than one fifth of the articles, with less attention to social skills during the first 12 volumes of *JABA*. Discrimination learning and cognitive skills constituted about 14% of the articles, with a drop in the proportion for the third time period. Measures of attention, on-task behavior, and engagement constituted about 12% of the articles, with the fewest occurring in the middle reporting period. Measures of other types of behaviors constituted relatively small proportions of the articles.

For measures of deceleration targets, definite shifts were seen across time. Unspecified or multiple aberrant behaviors of participants were measured relatively infrequently during the first and second time periods but increased to more than one fifth of the articles in the third reporting period. This pattern also is evident for self-injurious and aggressive behaviors. Emphasis on stereotypic behavior was high (26.1%) during the first 12 volumes but decreased substantially in the second and third time periods.

The independent variables used to influence the aforementioned categories of behaviors also were analyzed for the selected articles. Although these independent variables were used to increase a behavior, in some articles the authors also measured the effects on inappropriate behaviors (deceleration targets). The number and percentage of articles for these independent variables are displayed in Table 6. As shown, prompting of various types with reinforcement and analysis of reinforcers—including their quality, schedules, and so forth—were consistently used in a large percentage of the articles. Some independent variables were not used or used infrequently during the first time period (Vol-

TABLE 5
Number and Percentage of Articles by Categories of Behavior Across Three
Time Periods

Category of Behavior	Volumes 1–12[a] No. of Articles	%	Volumes 13–24[b] No. of Articles	%	Volumes 25–36[c] No. of Articles	%	All Volumes[d] No. of Articles	%
Accelerate behavior								
Language/communication	7	30.4	11	37.9	15	31.9	33	33.3
Social	3	13.0	7	24.1	12	25.5	22	22.2
Discrimination tasks and cognitive skills	4	17.4	6	20.7	4	8.5	14	14.1
Attention, on task, engagement	3	13.0	1	3.5	8	17.0	12	12.1
Play	3	13.0	1	3.5	1	2.1	5	5.1
Imitation	1	4.3	2	6.9	0	—	3	3.0
Compliance	1	4.3	1	3.5	0	—	2	2.0
Adaptive behavior	0	—	1	3.5	2	4.3	3	3.0
Affect	0	—	1	3.5	0	—	1	1.0
Behavioral techniques (adults)	1	4.3	1	3.5	0	—	2	2.0
Decelerate behavior								
Unspecified or multiple aberrant behaviors	1	4.3	1	3.5	10	21.3	12	12.1
Stereotypic (self-stimulatory) behaviors	6	26.1	1	3.5	2	4.3	9	9.1
Self-injurious behaviors	1	4.3	1	3.5	6	12.8	8	8.1
Disruptive behaviors	1	4.3	0	—	3	6.4	4	4.0
Aggressive behaviors	1	4.3	1	3.5	5	10.6	7	7.1
Destructive behaviors	0	—	0	—	2	4.3	2	2.0
Dangerous behaviors	1	4.3	0	—	0	—	1	1.0
Tantrums	1	4.3	0	—	0	—	1	1.0
Noncompliance	2	8.7	0	—	0	—	2	2.0
Seizures	1	4.3	0	—	0	—	1	1.0
Echolalia	1	4.3	2	6.9	0	—	3	3.0
Off task	0	—	1	3.5	0	—	1	1.0

Note. Many articles addressed multiple behaviors (e.g., multiple acceleration targets and multiple deceleration targets; numbers represent all those addressed).
[a]$n = 23$. [b]$n = 29$. [c]$n = 47$. [d]$n = 99$.

umes 1–12) but were used in the subsequent periods, including peer modeling and peer-mediated approaches, video modeling, self-management strategies, environmental arrangements, instructional packages and arrangements, and assessment packages. The opposite pattern is seen for token economies.

The independent variables used to decrease participants' behavior also were analyzed, and these data are shown in Table 7. Some definite patterns are noted in these data. Time-out, contingent aversive stimuli, and overcorrection were reported during the first 12 volumes of publication but were not used or used infrequently in the last 24 volumes. How-

TABLE 6
Number and Percentage of Independent Variables Used to Accelerate Behaviors

Independent Variable	Volumes 1–12[a]		Volumes 13–24[b]		Volumes 25–36[c]		All Volumes[d]	
	No. of Articles	%	No. of Articles	%	No. of Articles	%	No. of Articles	%
Prompts and reinforcement	5	21.7	14	48.3	5	10.6	24	24.2
Reinforcement (quality and schedules)	4	17.4	3	10.3	19	40.4	26	26.3
Peer modeling	0	—	1	3.5	1	2.1	2	2.0
Peer-mediated approaches	0	—	6	20.7	7	14.9	13	13.1
Token economy	3	13.0	1	3.5	0	—	4	4.0
Paced instructions	1	4.3	0	—	0	—	1	1.0
Stimulus shaping or fading	1	4.3	0	—	2	4.3	3	3.0
Video modeling	0	—	1	3.5	1	2.1	2	2.0
Self-management strategies	0	—	0	—	3	6.4	3	3.0
Facilitated communication	0	—	0	—	1	2.1	1	1.0
Modeling and instructions for adults	1	4.3	1	3.5	0	—	2	2.0
Environmental arrangements	2	8.7	6	20.7	8	17.0	16	16.2
Instructional arrangements and packages	0	—	6	20.7	8	17.0	14	14.1
Assessment strategies	0	—	0	—	6	12.8	6	6.1

Note.   Some articles used multiple independent variables; these numbers represent all that were used.
[a]$n = 23$. [b]$n = 29$. [c]$n = 47$. [d]$n = 99$.

ever, functional communication training, response interruption, and other more "positive" approaches (e.g., providing choices, interrupting responses) began to emerge during the last 12 volumes of publication. The articles also were analyzed to determine whether a functional analysis was reported. For the three time periods, the percentage of articles reporting a functional analysis was 8.7, 10.3, and 46.8, respectively. Thus, there is a marked increase in the proportion of articles including a functional analysis.

DISCUSSION

The purposes of this review were to describe the research including participants with autism published in *JABA* and to note changes occurring in the research over the journal's 36 volumes of publication. This was done with the assumption that the resulting data would describe the evolution of applied behavior analysis in the treatment of individuals with autism. From the review, the following five conclusions are noteworthy.

First, an increase was noted in the percentage of selected articles focusing on individuals with autism. Factors that may account for this increase include the increasing number of individuals diagnosed as having autism (National Research Council, 2001), in-

TABLE 7
Number and Percentage of Independent Variables Used to Decelerate Behaviors

Independent Variable	Volumes 1–12[a]		Volumes 13–24[b]		Volumes 25–36[c]		All Volumes[d]	
	No. of Articles	%	No. of Articles	%	No. of Articles	%	No. of Articles	%
Timeout	5	21.7	0	—	0	—	5	5.1
Extinction	1	4.3	0	—	5	10.6	6	6.1
DRO	2	8.7	0	—	1	2.1	3	3.0
Contingent aversive stimuli (e.g., shock, ammonia, restraint)	5	21.7	1	3.5	0	—	6	6.1
Overcorrection	6	26.1	0	—	0	—	6	6.1
Contingent exercise	0	—	1	3.5	1	2.1	2	2.0
Verbal reprimand	3	13.0	1	3.5	2	4.3	6	6.1
Functional communication training	0	—	0	—	8	17.0	8	8.1
Choice	0	—	0	—	1	2.1	1	1.0
Wearing weights	0	—	0	—	1	2.1	1	1.0
Response interruption	0	—	0	—	2	4.3	2	2.0

Note.   Some articles used multiple independent variables; these numbers represent all that were used. DRO = differential reinforcement of other behaviors.
[a]$n = 23$. [b]$n = 29$. [c]$n = 47$. [d]$n = 99$.

creased funding in autism treatment, or increased interest by behavioral researchers in autism. It is notable, however, for the field of autism treatment that nearly one quarter (24.7%) of the articles published in the last 12 volumes of *JABA* included participants with autism. *JABA* publishes a wide range of articles on a variety of topics; it is not a special education or disability specific periodical, and it does not focus specifically on educational interventions. Given there were 47 articles including participants with autism in the last 12 volumes of the journal, researchers and practitioners who are involved in autism treatment clearly should view *JABA* as a resource for their work. Further, as has been repeatedly shown, ABA is useful in devising and evaluating interventions for individuals with autism (Koegel & Koegel, 1995).

Second, relatively few of the selected articles were focused on family members, teachers, or other professionals working with individuals with autism. Despite the fact that most autism treatment programs (Handleman & Harris, 2000) include a parent involvement component, there appears to be relatively little research on this population. Further, despite work in helping siblings of children with other disabilities (e.g., Hancock & Kaiser, 1996), there were no reports of studies involving siblings of children with autism. Clearly, this is an area that may need additional investigation.

Third, from the selected articles, it appears that the autism treatment research is primarily focused on children 6 to 10 years of age in schools (see Tables 2 and 3). Although the percentage of participants with autism who are 5 years of age or younger or who are older adolescents and adults is increasing, the largest proportion of the reviewed research is more applicable to elementary school age children. In terms of the settings in which the research was conducted, much of it occurred in schools in separate classes including only individuals with disabilities or in therapy rooms located in the schools separate from other children. Although studies occurring in inclusive classes increased, the use of clinics and research laboratories constituted more than one fifth of the articles. Given the focus on natural environments and inclusive arrangements (Guralnick, 2001; Odom, 2002), the continued use of research labs and clinics raises questions about the extent to which the findings from the research are applicable where children are likely being served (i.e., in schools and homes). Strain, McGee, and Kohler (2001) described the existing rationale and myths related to including children with autism in educational programs. Although one fifth of the articles included a measure in a generalization setting, there clearly is a need for understanding how durable the effects of successful interventions are outside of the primary treatment context.

Fourth, much of the research focused on accelerating a target behavior or simultaneously measuring both acceleration and deceleration targets. Thus, autism treatment research published in *JABA* is not primarily devoted to addressing problematic behaviors. The types of behaviors measured for acceleration are predictable, in part, given the diagnostic criteria for individuals with autism. Specifically, language and communication skills and social skills were the two most frequently identified types of behaviors receiving intervention. Given the language/communication and social skill impairments of individuals with autism, this focus appears appropriate. Dawson and Osterling (1997) suggested the curriculum for individuals with autism should include (a) comprehension and use of language, (b) social skills and interaction, (c) attention to the environment (e.g., responding to multiple cues, engagement), (d) imitation of others, and (e) play. Others have suggested the curriculum should also include independence in usual routines and community participation (Marcus, Garfinkle, & Wolery, 2001). Relatively few of the selected articles addressed imitation of others, play, or adaptive behavior (independence and community participation). Clearly, a large literature exists on promoting language and communication skills (Goldstein, 2002) and social skills (McConnell, 2002), and it should be supplemented with research focusing on imitation, play, and adaptive behavior. The interventions to increase individuals' behavior reflected a reliance on known behavioral practices, including prompting and reinforcement. In later years, there was an increase in articles using environmental arrangements (e.g., structuring routines), instructional arrangements (e.g., using varied instructional tasks), and instructional packages (embedding instruction in other activities), and involving peers in the application of the intervention. These tend to be consistent with recommended practices, at least for children up to 8 years of age (Sandall, McLean, & Smith, 2000).

Fifth, although much of the research focused on accelerating behavior, a sizable portion focused on the reduction of behavior. In terms of behaviors measured, there was an increase over the years of studies focusing on multiple challenging behaviors and of studies focusing on self-injurious and aggressive behaviors. There was a decrease over the years of studies focused specifically on stereotypic behaviors. Dramatic changes occurred in the nature of the independent variables used for challenging behaviors. There was a decrease in the use of contingent aversive stimuli and overcorrection and an increase in the use of functional communication training and reinforcement (including extinction) studies. Likewise, in the last 12 years there was a sharp increase in the use of functional assessments of problematic behaviors. This reflects the general trend to the use of positive behavior supports (Lucyshyn, Dunlap, & Albin, 2002) and with a broader synthesis of research on challenging behaviors (Horner, Carr, Strain, Todd, & Reed, 2002).

This article includes several limitations. We used a broad definition of autism, and from the data collected we cannot determine whether all participants identified as having autism would meet current diagnostic criteria. Our review included only two of the four issues for each volume of *JABA;* had all issues been reviewed, a different picture of the trends across time may have been noted. In addition, the review was restricted to *JABA.* As noted earlier, treatment research studies in autism, including ABA treatment studies, are published in a large number of journals (e.g., Schreibman, 2000). It is unclear from this review whether analyzing articles from other periodicals would have presented a different picture of autism treatment research. Similarly, from the data collected, we cannot argue that each included article exemplified the dimensions of ABA as defined by Baer et al. (1968). Nonetheless, the conclusions drawn from this review show a partial picture of how ABA research related to individuals with autism has changed over the last three decades. In addition, the review suggests there are significant areas for future research in understanding precisely what ABA has to offer families of individuals with autism.

ACKNOWLEDGMENTS

This article was supported in part by U.S. Department of Education Grant H325A030093. The opinions expressed do not necessarily reflect the policy of the U.S. Department of Education, and no official endorsement by the U.S. Department of Education should be inferred.

REFERENCES

Baer, D. M., Wolf, M. M., & Risley, T. R. (1968). Some current dimensions of applied behavior analysis. *Journal of Applied Behavior Analysis, 1,* 91–97.

Dawson, G., & Osterling, J. (1997). Early intervention in autism. In M. J. Guralnick (Ed.), *The effectiveness of early intervention* (pp. 307–326). Baltimore: Brookes.

Goldstein, H. (2002). Communication intervention for children with autism: A review of treatment efficacy. *Journal of Autism and Developmental Disorders, 32,* 373–396.

Guralnick, M. J. (2001). *Early childhood inclusion: Focus on change.* Baltimore: Brookes.

Hancock, T. B., & Kaiser, A. P. (1996). Siblings use of milieu teaching at home. *Topics in Early Childhood Special Education, 16,* 168–190.

Handleman, J. S., & Harris, S. L. (2000). *Preschool education programs for children with autism* (2nd ed.). Austin, TX: Pro-Ed.

Horner, R. H., Carr, E. G., Strain, P. S., Todd, A. W., & Reed, H. K. (2002). Problem behavior interventions for young children with autism: A research synthesis. *Journal of Autism and Developmental Disorders, 32,* 423–446.

Kanner, L. (1943). Autistic disturbances of affective contact. *Nervous Child, 2,* 217–250.

Koegel, R. L., & Koegel, L. K. (1995). *Teaching children with autism.* Baltimore: Brookes.

Lucyshyn, J. M., Dunlap, G., & Albin, R. W. (2002). *Families and positive behavior support: Addressing problem behavior in family contexts.* Baltimore: Brookes.

Marcus, L. M., Garfinkle, A., & Wolery, M. (2001). Issues in early diagnosis and intervention in young children with autism. In E. Schopler & N. Yirmiya (Eds.), *The research basis for autism intervention* (pp. 171–185). New York: Kluwer/Plenum.

McConnell, S. R. (2002). Interventions to facilitate social interaction for young children with autism: Review of available research and recommendations for educational intervention and future research. *Journal of Autism and Developmental Disorders, 32,* 351–372.

National Research Council, Division of Behavioral and Social Sciences and Education, Committee on Educational Interventions for Children with Autism. (2001). *Educating children with autism.* Washington, DC: National Academy Press.

Odom, S. L. (2002). *Widening the circle: Including children with disabilities in preschool programs.* New York: Teachers College Press.

Sandall, S., McLean, M., & Smith, B. (2000). *DEC recommended practices in early intervention/early childhood special education.* Longmont, CO: Sporis West.

Schreibman, L. (2000). Intensive behavioral/psychoeducational treatments for autism: Research needs and future directions. *Journal of Autism and Developmental Disorders, 30,* 373–378.

Schwartz, I., Billingsley, F. F., & Wolery, M. (1999). Letters to the editor. *Infants and Young Children, 11*(3), xii–xiii.

Strain, P. S., McGee, G. G., & Kohler, F. W. (2001). Inclusion of children with autism in early intervention environments. In M. J. Guralnick (Ed.), *Early childhood inclusion: Focus on change* (pp. 337–363). Baltimore: Brookes.

EXCEPTIONALITY, *13*(1), 25–34

Implications of Functional Analysis Methodology for the Design of Intervention Programs

Brian A. Iwata
Department of Psychology
University of Florida

April S. Worsdell
Rehabilitation Institute
Southern Illinois University

Functional analysis methodology is an assessment strategy that identifies sources of reinforcement that maintain problem behavior and prescribes individualized interventions that directly alter the conditions under which behavior occurs. In this article we describe the environmental determinants of problem behavior, methods for conducting functional analyses, and implications for the design of intervention programs.

Functional analysis methodology is one of the most significant developments in research on behavior disorders over the past 25 years and is now considered best practice. Functional analysis is an assessment strategy that identifies the environmental determinants of behavior (i.e., its functional characteristics). For individuals with autism who display challenging behavior, functional analysis serves as an excellent strategy to inform clinical decision making so that interventions can be developed to alter specific features of the environment that influence an individual's behavior. This article presents an overview of functional analysis methodology and its implications for the design of intervention programs.

SOURCES OF REINFORCEMENT FOR PROBLEM BEHAVIOR

Results of numerous studies indicate that most problem behaviors are learned as a result of an individual's experience with his or her environment and are maintained by contin-

Requests for reprints should be sent to Brian A. Iwata, Department of Psychology, University of Florida, 114 Psychology Building, P.O. Box 112250, Gainesville, FL 32611–2250. E-mail: iwata@ufl.edu

gencies of reinforcement. Although specific reinforcers for problem behavior may vary widely, for the purpose of developing treatment it has been convenient to consider positive and negative reinforcement as the two fundamental contingencies that maintain behavior and to further classify these based on whether reinforcement is delivered by other persons (social) or is a direct (automatic) result of the behavior.

Positive Reinforcement

Lovaas and Simmons (1969) presented data indicating that attention from caring adults, when delivered contingent on the occurrence of self-injurious behavior (SIB), increased the frequency of the behavior. The occurrence of a serious problem behavior, such as SIB, aggression, or property destruction, often produces a variety of reactions from caregivers: response interruption, reprimands, comfort, or attempts to redirect the person's behavior. Often unavoidable, these consequences may interrupt problem behavior temporarily but actually increase its occurrence over time as a result of *social-positive reinforcement*. By contrast, other behaviors (some forms of stereotypy or SIB) persist in the absence of any social stimulation (Berkson & Mason, 1963). A common characteristic of these behaviors is that they are maintained by sensory consequences, which are directly produced by the behavior through a process that has been described as *automatic-positive reinforcement* (Vaughan & Michael, 1982).

Negative Reinforcement

Problem behavior also may result in the termination of ongoing activity. For example, some individuals are not required to complete academic tasks or to even attend class because their behavior is so dangerous or disruptive. Although sometimes viewed as a form of "time out," these consequences may actually produce escape from work and strengthen behavior through *social-negative reinforcement* (Iwata, 1987). Finally, some responses directly terminate or at least attenuate ongoing stimulation (e.g., rubbing the temples when one has a headache or scratching the site of an insect bite). These behaviors may intensify when alternative responses (such as taking medicine) are not available and may recur whenever pain is experienced. This type of *automatic-negative reinforcement* usually applies only to SIB, and even then rarely.

FUNCTIONAL ANALYSIS METHODOLOGY

The purpose of a functional analysis (sometimes called a functional behavioral assessment) is to determine which of the aforementioned contingencies maintains an individual's problem behavior. Three general approaches to assessment have been reported in the literature; each is described briefly next (see Iwata, Kahng, Wallace, & Lindberg, 2000, for an extensive review). The approaches differ in terms of the type of data that are collected and the extent to which environmental events are merely observed or actually manipulated during the course of assessment. Despite these variations, all have in common an attempt to identify the antecedent events that occasion behavior and the consequent events that serve as reinforcers.

Anecdotal or Indirect Methods

A number of structured interviews and checklists have been developed to solicit information about situations in which problem behavior occurs. The Motivation Assessment Scale (MAS; Durand & Crimmins, 1988) is an example of a commonly used instrument. The scale consists of 16 questions about the circumstances under which problem behavior may or may not occur, and answers are provided by circling a number ranging from 0 (*never*) to 6 (*always*). The numeric values are summed or averaged to yield a total for each of four possible functions: positive reinforcement through attention, positive reinforcement through access to materials, negative reinforcement through escape, or "sensory" (i.e., automatic-positive) reinforcement. (Note that pain attenuation or automatic-negative reinforcement is not included in the MAS.)

The primary advantage of indirect methods is their simplicity and efficiency: Assessment occurs during the course of an interview and takes only a few minutes. However, because the data consist solely of verbal report, which can be inaccurate for a number of reasons, these methods have been found to be unreliable (Sturmey, 1994). Therefore, they should be used only as preliminary information-gathering devices and should not serve as the basis for developing intervention plans.

Descriptive (Correlational) Analysis

This approach involves direct observation of behavior and the environmental situations in which it occurs (Bijou, Peterson, & Ault, 1968). The most common form of descriptive analysis is known as *A-B-C recording* (A—antecedent, B—behavior, C—consequence), in which an observer enters data whenever problem behavior occurs: time and setting, problem behavior, and events occurring immediately prior to and following the target behavior (Sulzer-Azaroff & Mayer, 1977). An alternative method, known as *interval recording,* involves using an observational code to mark the presence or absence of specific antecedents, behaviors, and consequences during brief time intervals (e.g., 10 sec) and is typically used to assess high-rate behaviors (Mace & Lalli, 1991). Data gathered using either method are summarized as conditional probabilities based on observed frequencies of events (e.g., the number of times that aggression was preceded by instructions, or the number of times that SIB was followed by attention). Inferences about maintaining variables are based on observed correlations between problem behavior and its antecedents or consequences.

Because the descriptive analysis is based on direct observation rather than on informant recall, it is far superior to the indirect approach and is perhaps the most frequently used method of assessment. Nevertheless, the descriptive analysis has certain limitations because it does not allow control over the environmental contexts in which behavior occurs. As a result, the occurrence of problem behavior may be related to multiple events (as in escape from tasks accompanied by teacher attention), any one of which could account for behavioral maintenance. In addition, data may not reveal relationships between behavior and intermittent sources of reinforcement that result in low conditional probabilities.

Functional (Experimental) Analysis

When descriptive analysis yields ambiguous results, a functional analysis may be conducted to allow systematic introduction and removal of environmental events during predefined test and control conditions. Iwata, Dorsey, Slifer, Bauman, and Richman (1982/1994) described a general model consisting of three test conditions and one control. In the attention condition, a therapist is present but does not interact with the individual except to deliver attention following occurrences of problem behavior (test for social-positive reinforcement function). In the demand condition, a therapist presents learning tasks to the individual but allows the individual to escape a trial following the occurrence of problem behavior (test for social-negative reinforcement). In the alone condition, the individual is observed in a relatively barren environment (test for automatic-positive reinforcement). These conditions, unlike those commonly encountered in the natural environment, separate the different sources of reinforcement that might maintain behavior. (Note that there is no test condition for automatic-negative reinforcement, which would require exposing the individual to pain or discomfort.) Rates of behavior observed during these conditions are compared to those in a play (control) condition, in which the individual has free access to leisure items and social interaction throughout the session. High rates of behavior in one test condition, relative to others and the control, identify the functional characteristics of behavior by revealing the environmental events responsible for its occurrence. A number of variations of this model been developed over the years (see Hanley, Iwata, & McCord, 2003, for a review), including a "brief functional analysis," which can be completed during the course of an outpatient evaluation (Northup et al., 1991).

The major advantage of the functional analysis is that it is the only approach to assessment that identifies cause–effect relations. In addition, its flexibility allows one to examine the influence of numerous and potentially subtle variables on behavior (e.g., certain types of task demands). The most significant limitation of the functional analysis is that it is the most complex form of assessment, requiring therapists to maintain a high degree of consistency in implementing assessment conditions. Other limitations include the fact that it may not be appropriate for the assessment of behavior that poses a high degree of risk or behavior that occurs at extremely low rates.

DESIGN OF INTERVENTION PROGRAMS

Research in applied behavior analysis has led to the development of a wide range of reinforcement-based procedures for reducing the frequency of problem behavior. These procedures have proliferated to the point where it may be difficult to identify the essential features of a given intervention because researchers typically emphasize its novel characteristics. In actuality, most if not all reinforcement-based interventions decrease behavior by (a) altering antecedent conditions to make behavior less susceptible to reinforcement, (b) eliminating reinforcement for the behavior, or (c) reinforcing the absence of problem behavior or the occurrence of an alternative behavior. These three processes reduce behavior in fundamentally different ways and therefore represent the most common denominators of all reinforcement-based interventions. Although other components of treatment also may be important in particular situations, they are, by and large, procedural details, and to attempt to learn every variation of every procedure would be an impossible task. Moreover, familiarity with a large number of "techniques" without knowledge of their underlying basis for behavior change makes it difficult to modify a procedure systematically when it does not work.

The task of designing a reinforcement-based intervention thus becomes one of determining which antecedent conditions to change, how to limit reinforcement for problem behavior, and how to strengthen alternative behavior. The information provided by a functional analysis is essential in making these determinations. In addition to suggesting strategies for effectively reducing behavior, the results of a functional analysis allow us to determine, on an a priori basis, which interventions are likely to be ineffective. In the following sections, we illustrate each of the three approaches just noted for different functions of problem behavior.

Alteration of Antecedent Events: Establishing Operations and Noncontingent Reinforcement

The influence of antecedent events on behavior has been recognized for many years and has been described using a variety of terms, including contextual or ecological variables, setting events, and stimulus control. The most thorough treatment of antecedent events has been provided by Michael (Laraway, Snycerski, Michael, & Poling, 2003; Michael, 2000). He noted that behavior maintained by reinforcement occurs because the presence of some antecedent event makes a reinforcer valuable and indicated that any antecedent that alters the effectiveness (value) of a reinforcer is an establishing operation (EO). The most common EO for behavior maintained by positive reinforcement is deprivation (e.g., from food or water); the typical EO for behavior maintained by negative reinforcement is aversive stimulation (e.g., intense light, noise). The effects of EOs are diminished when responding produces reinforcement, as in attention-getting behavior that ceases when attention is delivered (positive reinforcement) or as in aggression that stops when it produces escape (negative reinforcement), but EOs also can be attenuated prior to responding merely by providing noncontingent access to the reinforcer.

Using noncontingent reinforcement (NCR) as the basis for behavior change, specific procedures can be formulated for different sources of reinforcement. NCR for problem behavior maintained by social-positive reinforcement (e.g., attention) would consist of a richer schedule of noncontingent attention. After determining that the SIB of three individuals was maintained by attention, Vollmer, Iwata, Zarcone, Smith, and Mazaleski (1993) initially delivered noncontingent attention on an almost continuous schedule (every 10 sec) and observed marked reductions in SIB. SIB remained low as the schedule was gradually thinned until it reached 5 min, which was determined to be practical for implementation. Similar procedures have been used to decrease problem behavior maintained by automatic-positive reinforcement. For example, Piazza, Adelinis, Hanley, Goh, and Delia (2000) identified leisure items that delivered stimulation similar to that produced by stereotypy and SIB and observed large reductions in these behaviors when the items were made available noncontingently.

Because the EO for escape behavior (social-negative reinforcement) often involves presentation of an aversive task, NCR for such behavior would entail noncontingent task removal or modification, which can be accomplished in several ways: Weeks and Gaylord-Ross (1981) reduced task complexity by substituting easy tasks in place of difficult ones; Pace, Iwata, Cowdery, Andree, and McIntyre (1996) initially reduced task frequency by placing fewer demands on participants; and Vollmer, Marcus, and Ringdahl (1995) provided noncontingent breaks from work tasks. Finally, problem behavior maintained by pain attenuation (automatic-negative reinforcement) provides the most obvious example supporting the use of NCR, which involves removing the discomfort that serves as the EO. This approach to treatment has been described anecdotally but has not been demonstrated empirically, most likely due to difficulties in assessing pain (and its reduction) in individuals who have severe communication deficits.

Interventions based solely on the alteration of EOs do not affect the reinforcement contingency responsible for maintaining the behavior problem; rather, they make reinforcement less valuable. Thus, the main advantage of NCR is that it may reduce problem behavior even though reinforcement for problem behavior is still available, making it a particularly attractive option when extinction is not feasible (discussed next). On the other hand, problem behavior is likely to recur if it continues to be reinforced, especially at times when NCR is not present. Therefore, the elimination of reinforcement for problem behavior should be an important component of intervention.

Discontinuation of Reinforcement: Extinction

Extinction—the reduction of behavior by withholding reinforcement—is an easily understood principle but one that is difficult to implement for two reasons. First, extinction requires that the behavior be allowed to continue, which may not be feasible if the behavior occurs at high intensity. Second, the typical extinction procedure, "planned ignoring," assumes that attention is the maintaining reinforcer for problem behavior (hence, the withholding of attention). Because problem behavior may be maintained by multiple sources of reinforcement, the procedures that define extinction in a given situation are determined by the specific nature of reinforcement to be discontinued.

Extinction for behavior maintained by attention and other forms of social-positive reinforcement involves the withholding of positive reinforcement, which often has taken the form of not reacting to the behavior or terminating ongoing interaction when the behavior occurs (Liberman, Teigen, Patterson, & Baker, 1973). Although this form of extinction is commonly recommended as treatment for a wide range of behavior problems, rarely has it been used as the sole means of intervention. In most research on the treatment of problem behavior, extinction has been combined with other procedures such as NCR (discussed previously) or differential reinforcement (discussed next).

Extinction procedures for behavior maintained by automatic-positive reinforcement are more difficult to develop because the specific reinforcers directly produced by the behavior usually cannot be seen or controlled. Nevertheless, when it is possible to identify a behavior's automatic reinforcers, extinction might be implemented by arranging conditions so that the behavior's consequences are attenuated. This form of extinction has been called *sensory extinction* and has been applied to stereotypy (Rincover, Cook, Peoples, & Packard, 1979) as well as SIB (Dorsey, Iwata, Reid, & Davis, 1982). The procedure often entails mechanical intervention that disrupts the stimulation produced by a behavior but that does not interfere with the behavior per se. Examples include padding walls or furniture, or having individuals wear padded equipment.

Results of a functional analysis are particularly important when considering the use of extinction with escape behavior (social-negative reinforcement). To the extent that the "ignoring" variant of extinction involves cessation of interaction, it will serve as inadvertent negative reinforcement and will exacerbate the problem. Extinction of escape is achieved through continued presentation of the EO for problem behavior (e.g., work tasks and related instructions) and *not* removing these activities contingent on the occurrence of problem behavior (Iwata, Pace, Kalsher, Cowdery, & Cataldo, 1990; Steege, Wacker, Berg, Cigrand, & Cooper, 1989).

The final case for which extinction might be considered consists of behavior (usually SIB) maintained by its pain-attenuating consequences (automatic-negative reinforcement). Aside from the fact that it would be very difficult to arrange a situation in which behavior does not terminate ongoing stimulation (e.g., as in scratching that does not relieve an itch), there is little justification for this type of extinction because it leaves the individual with no effective means of dealing with the problem. Furthermore, the elimination of such behavior through extinction may reduce caregivers' ability to determine that the individual is, in fact, in need of physical intervention or medical attention.

Differential Reinforcement

Although treatment procedures based on NCR and extinction can be highly effective in reducing problem behavior, they do not explicitly strengthen alternative behaviors that are either less dangerous or more socially acceptable. Behavioral replacement of this type is achieved through differential reinforcement of other behavior (DRO) and differential reinforcement of alternative behavior (DRA), and several variations of both procedures have been reported in the literature (see Vollmer & Iwata, 1992, for a review). Because DRO involves delivering reinforcement for the nonoccurrence of behavior during some interval of time, the procedure is somewhat similar to extinction in that appropriate behavior is not directly shaped. In fact, results of a study by Mazaleski, Iwata, Vollmer, Zarcone, and Smith (1993) indicated that the behavior-reducing effects of DRO were primarily a function of the extinction component and not the reinforcement component of the contingency. Therefore, emphasis here is placed on DRA procedures.

Day, Rea, Schussler, Larsen, and Johnson (1988) described an interesting application of DRA as treatment for SIB maintained by access to leisure items (social-positive reinforcement). Treatment consisted of making these items unobtainable following SIB but available following the occurrence of specific vocal and gestural responses. This strategy, in which extinction is combined with differential reinforcement for appropriate "requesting" behavior, also has been used commonly to reduce problem behavior maintained by attention (Durand & Carr, 1992). Similar types of consequences (access to leisure items) may be used to reduce problem behavior maintained by automatic-positive reinforcement. Here, however, a DRA intervention will be effective only to the extent that access to the leisure items is preferred over stimulation produced by the problem behavior. If not, additional techniques, such as prompting and reinforcing appropriate behavior, or blocking problem behavior, may be required (Lindberg, Iwata, & Kahng, 1999).

Differential reinforcement as treatment for problem behavior maintained by social-negative reinforcement has taken several forms. First, more potent positive reinforcement than that currently available can be used to strengthen the alternative behavior. Mace and Belfiore (1990) used this approach to increase compliance with instructions and decrease escape. They first identified instructions for which there was a high probability of compliance. When these were presented in a 3:1 ratio with instructions for which compliance was low, escape behavior decreased and compliance increased. A second approach involves negative reinforcement (i.e., a break from the task, avoidance of prompts, etc.) instead of positive reinforcement made contingent on compliance (Iwata et al., 1990). A third example of DRA involves reinforcement of alternative escape behaviors. Steege et al. (1990) used such an approach while treating two individuals who exhibited SIB in training situations. Contingent on pressing a microswitch (activating a tape recorder that played the word *stop*), brief breaks from training were provided.

DRA procedures applied to pain-attenuating behavior (automatic-negative reinforcement) would involve establishing responses that reduce discomfort. Individuals initially might be taught an alternative behavior indicating a painful condition, which would be reinforced by having someone alleviate the discomfort (negative reinforcement). The focus of intervention might subsequently be shifted to teach a response (self-medication) that directly reduces pain. These behaviors may be difficult to establish because the ideal context (the presence of pain) for teaching the alternative response may not occur frequently.

SUMMARY

Research conducted over the past 25 years has indicated that most problem behaviors are acquired and maintained through contingencies of reinforcement. Therefore, analysis of the structural characteristics of behavior (what it looks like) is less likely to yield information relevant to treatment than is the analysis of its functional characteristics (what maintains it). Functional analysis methodology identifies sources of reinforcement that maintain problem behavior and, in turn, identifies those features of the environment that need to be changed to reduce problem behavior. More specifically, the outcome of a functional analysis will suggest strategies for designing intervention programs that can change behavior in three fundamental ways: altering antecedent events (establishing operations) to make behavior less susceptible to reinforcement (NCR), eliminating the reinforcement for problem behavior (extinction), and strengthening alternative responses (differential reinforcement).

ACKNOWLEDGMENT

Preparation of this article was supported in part through a grant from the Florida Department of Children and Families.

REFERENCES

Berkson, G., & Mason, W. A. (1963). Stereotyped movements of mental defectives: Three situational effects. *American Journal of Mental Deficiency, 68,* 409–412.

Bijou, S. W., Peterson, R. F., & Ault, M. H. (1968). A method to integrate descriptive and experimental field studies at the level of data and empirical concepts. *Journal of Applied Behavior Analysis, 1,* 175–191.

Day, R. M., Rea, J. A., Schussler, N. G., Larsen, S. E., & Johnson, W. L. (1988). A functionally based approach to the treatment of self-injurious behavior. *Behavior Modification, 12,* 565–589.

Dorsey, M. F., Iwata, B. A., Reid, D. H., & Davis, P. A. (1982). Protective equipment: Continuous and contingent application in the treatment of self-injurious behavior. *Journal of Applied Behavior Analysis, 15,* 217–230.

Durand, V. M., & Carr, E. G. (1992). An analysis of maintenance following functional communication training. *Journal of Applied Behavior Analysis, 25,* 777–794.

Durand, V. M., & Crimmins, D. B. (1988). Identifying the variables maintaining self-injurious behavior. *Journal of Autism and Developmental Disorders, 18,* 99–117.

Hanley, G. P., Iwata, B. A., & McCord, B. E. (2003). Functional analysis of problem behavior: A review. *Journal of Applied Behavior Analysis, 36,* 147–186.

Iwata, B. A. (1987). Negative reinforcement in applied behavior analysis: An emerging technology. *Journal of Applied Behavior Analysis, 20,* 361–387.

Iwata, B. A., Dorsey, M. F., Slifer, K. J., Bauman, K. E., & Richman, G. S. (1994). Toward a functional analysis of self-injury. *Journal of Applied Behavior Analysis, 27,* 197–209. (Reprinted from *Analysis and Intervention in Developmental Disabilities, 2,* 3–20, 1982)

Iwata, B. A., Kahng, S., Wallace, M. D., & Lindberg, J. S. (2000). The functional analysis model of behavioral assessment. In J. Austin & J. E. Carr (Eds.), *Handbook of applied behavior analysis* (pp. 61–89). Reno, NV: Context Press.

Iwata, B. A., Pace, G. M., Kalsher, M. J., Cowdery, G. E., & Cataldo, M. F. (1990). Experimental analysis and extinction of self-injurious escape behavior. *Journal of Applied Behavior Analysis, 23,* 11–27.

Laraway, S., Snycerski, S., Michael, J., & Poling, A. (2003). Motivating operations and terms to describe them: Some further refinements. *Journal of Applied Behavior Analysis, 36,* 407–414.

Liberman, R. P., Teigen, J., Patterson, R., & Baker, V. (1973). Reducing delusional speech in chronic paranoid schizophrenics. *Journal of Applied Behavior Analysis, 6,* 57–64.

Lindberg, J. S., Iwata, B. A., & Kahng, S. (1999). On the relation between object manipulation and stereotypic self-injurious behavior. *Journal of Applied Behavior Analysis, 32,* 51–62.

Lovaas, O. I., & Simmons, J. Q. (1969). Manipulation of self-destruction in three retarded children. *Journal of Applied Behavior Analysis, 2,* 143–157.

Mace, F. C., & Belfiore, P. (1990). Behavioral momentum in the treatment of escape-motivated stereotypy. *Journal of Applied Behavior Analysis, 23,* 507–514.

Mace, F. C., & Lalli, J. S. (1991). Linking descriptive and experimental analyses in the treatment of bizarre speech. *Journal of Applied Behavior Analysis, 24,* 553–562.

Mazaleski, J. L., Iwata, B. A., Vollmer, T. R., Zarcone, J. R., & Smith, R. G. (1993). Analysis of the reinforcement and extinction components in differential reinforcement of other behavior (DRO) contingencies with self-injury. *Journal of Applied Behavior Analysis, 26,* 143–156.

Michael, J. (2000). Implications and refinements of the establishing operation concept. *Journal of Applied Behavior Analysis, 33,* 401–410.

Northup, J., Wacker, D., Sasso, G., Steege, M., Cigrand, K., Cook, J., et al. (1991). A brief functional analysis of aggressive and alternative behavior in an outclinic setting. *Journal of Applied Behavior Analysis, 24,* 509–522.

Pace, G. M., Iwata, B. A., Cowdery, G. E., Andree, P. J., & McIntyre, T. (1996). Stimulus (instructional) fading during extinction of self-injurious escape behavior. *Journal of Applied Behavior Analysis, 26,* 205–212.

Piazza, C. C., Adelinis, J. D., Hanley, G. P., Goh, H., & Delia, M. D. (2000). An evaluation of the effects of matched stimuli on behaviors maintained by automatic reinforcement. *Journal of Applied Behavior Analysis, 33,* 13–27.

Rincover, A., Cook, R., Peoples, A., & Packard, D. (1979). Sensory extinction and sensory reinforcement principles for programming multiple adaptive behavior change. *Journal of Applied Behavior Analysis, 12,* 221–233.

Steege, M. W., Wacker, D. P., Berg, W. K., Cigrand, K. K., & Cooper, L. J. (1989). The use of behavioral assessment to prescribe and evaluate treatments for severely handicapped children. *Journal of Applied Behavior Analysis, 22,* 23–33.

Steege, M. W., Wacker, D. P., Cigrand, K. C., Berg, W. K., Novak, C. G., Reimers, T. M., et al. (1990). Use of negative reinforcement in the treatment of self-injurious behavior. *Journal of Applied Behavior Analysis, 23,* 459–467.

Sturmey, P. (1994). Assessing the functions of aberrant behaviors: A review of psychometric instruments. *Journal of Autism and Developmental Disorders, 24,* 293–304.

Sulzer-Azaroff, B., & Mayer, G. R. (1977). *Applying behavior-analysis procedures with children and youth.* New York: Holt, Rinehart & Winston.

Vaughan, M. E., & Michael, J. (1982). Automatic reinforcement: An important but ignored concept. *Behaviorism, 10,* 217–227.

Vollmer, T. R., & Iwata, B. A. (1992). Differential reinforcement as treatment for behavior disorders: Procedural and functional variations. *Research in Developmental Disabilities, 13,* 393–417.

Vollmer, T. R., Iwata, B. A., Zarcone, J. R., Smith, R. G., & Mazaleski, J. L. (1993). The role of attention in the treatment of attention-maintained self-injurious behavior: Noncontingent reinforcement (NCR) and differential reinforcement of other behavior (DRO). *Journal of Applied Behavior Analysis, 26,* 9–21.

Vollmer, T. R., Marcus, B. A., & Ringdahl, J. E. (1995). Noncontingent escape as treatment for self-injurious behavior maintained by negative reinforcement. *Journal of Applied Behavior Analysis, 28,* 15–26.

Weeks, M., & Gaylord-Ross, R. (1981). Task difficulty and aberrant behavior in severely handicapped students. *Journal of Applied Behavior Analysis, 14,* 449–463.

EXCEPTIONALITY, *13*(1), 35–44
Copyright © 2005, Lawrence Erlbaum Associates, Inc.

Potential Applications of Behavioral Fluency for Students With Autism

Richard M. Kubina, Jr. and Pamela Wolfe
Department of Educational and School Psychology and Special Education
Pennsylvania State University

Curricula for students with autism do not take into account levels of learning such as behavioral fluency. Behavioral fluency addresses accuracy as well as speed of response. We posit that fluency increases the functionality of skills for students with autism and should be systematically programmed into a curriculum. To discuss the application of fluency for students with autism, we present background related to response competence, critical learning outcomes associated with behavioral fluency, and how fluency fits into a hierarchy of learning. We apply the concept of behavioral fluency to individuals with autism and suggest that research continue.

The lifelong consequences of autism create a need for a wide range of effective educational and therapeutic programs. One of the most critical variables in effective education is the curriculum. As a scope and sequence of instruction, a good curriculum designates what students will learn and in what order (Engelmann, 1997). A curriculum identifies the terminal skills the student will display at the end of a program, allowing teachers to program instruction and monitor progress. An effective curriculum-based program for students with autism should result in functional behaviors, age-appropriate skills, and present connections within (e.g., adding basic math facts and later applying that skill to addition facts with regrouping) and across (e.g., a social skill like greeting people and a vocational skill like working at a cash register) curricular domains (Scheuermann & Webber, 2002). Good curricula function like a road map, providing the teacher with clear directions to a final destination. Currently available curricula, however, do not take into account levels of learning such as fluency. We posit that fluency increases the functionality of skills for students with autism and should be systematically programmed into a curriculum.

Requests for reprints should be sent to Richard M. Kubina, Jr., Department of Educational and School Psychology and Special Education, Pennsylvania State University, University Park, PA 16802. E-mail: rmk11@psu.edu

BEHAVIORAL FLUENCY DEFINED

In general, the term *fluency* has entered into the vernacular for most people. When asking someone to provide synonyms for *fluency* (e.g., to describe a fluent speaker, dancer, or writer), words such as *smooth, flowing, accurate, graceful, automatic,* and *effortless* may be given. On a descriptive level such words capture the essence of fluency. A student who reads fluently is easily recognized from a student who does not. A child who speaks fluently sounds quite different from a child who has English as his or her second language or is learning to speak. In both cases, descriptors for dysfluent language behavior might include *halting, inaccurate,* and *slow.* Commonalties between words for fluency and dysfluency encompass accuracy and speed at which a person can perform a behavior. Although a number of researchers in education have studied fluency, basic observations supporting behavioral fluency came from an approach called Precision Teaching (PT). Explanations of the PT method fall beyond the scope of this article; however, many fluency articles have their empirical roots in PT.

Although researchers need to continue examining methods and variables responsible for the outcome of the fluency, the evidence base showing the positive effects of behavioral fluency is compelling (Beck & Clement, 1991; Binder, 1996; Johnson & Layng, 1992; Kubina & Morrison, 2000; Maloney, 1998). For example, Haughton (1972) observed that when students could answer basic math facts at about 40 to 50 digits per minute, they could learn more complex problems later in the curriculum sequence. The rate of answering 40 to 50 digit problems correctly, not just getting 100% correct, allowed the students to use those basic math facts fluently with advanced skills predicated on basic math fact fluency (e.g., complex addition—multiple digit problems with regrouping). Across time, individual and entire school performances have shown how fluency enhances student performance.

To discuss the application of fluency for students with autism, we present background related to response competence. Second, we explore critical learning outcomes associated with behavioral fluency and how fluency fits into a hierarchy of learning. Finally, we apply the concept of behavioral fluency to individuals with autism.

LEVELS OF LEARNING

Learning may be characterized as having several levels or stages indicating the degree of competence a student has obtained: acquisition, fluency, maintenance, and generalization (proposed by Alberto & Troutman, 2003). The first level of response competency is the acquisition stage or level that centers on the goal of accuracy (Mercer & Mercer, 2001). Differing levels of response competence means the behavior learned varies in functionality. For instance, a student who can identify eight colors at 100% accuracy may be said to have acquired color labeling. Although the student has attained accuracy, his competence with the acquired task may be questionable. For example, a student who can label eight out of eight colors correctly in 20 sec performs the behavior much more competently than a student who needs 1 min to correctly label the same eight colors.

Fluency means the student is both accurate and fast (Howell & Lorson-Howell, 1990). A student who labels colors fluently does so accurately but also with speed.

Asking a student "What color is this?" will result in an immediate correct response if she or he has attained fluency. The fluency or proficiency level's goal centers on the automatic performance of a skill (Mercer & Mercer, 2001; Wolery, Jones-Ault, & Munson-Doyle, 1992).

The next level of the response competence hierarchy, maintenance, suggests that a behavior will occur for an extended period of time without having to reteach the skill. A student who forgets the answer to a math fact like $1 + 1 = 2$ will require additional review. By having to reteach a previously learned skill, the teacher and student lose instructional time that might otherwise be spent on new learning. If multiple skills require reteaching, the student's overall progress is considerably hindered.

At the peak of the hierarchy is generalization, or using a skill in situations different from acquisition. A teacher who had an initial instructional set of triangles could test for generalization by asking the student to identify triangles varying in degrees of shape, color, and spatial orientation (Engelmann, 1997). A skill that shows generalization allows the student to capitalize on the instruction and respond effectively in situations involving novel stimuli. Without generalization a student limits himself or herself to making responses matching the instructional set, a skill sure to encumber the student's future learning progress.

The relationships among the levels of response competence are not independent but interactive. Starting at the acquisition level, a student must firmly establish a response before she or he can attain accuracy and speed, or fluency. For maintenance, or long-term retention, the student must reach the fluency level. Without maintenance, the student will not generalize a skill beyond the initial instruction. An extensive amount of research describes varying curricula and successful approaches to acquisition for students with autism (e.g., Frost & Bondy, 1994; Leaf & McEachin, 1998; Maurice, Green, & Luce, 1996; Sundberg & Partington, 1998). In addition, approaches for producing maintenance and generalization of skills for students with autism exist (e.g., Dunlap, 1984; Lovaas, 2003; Maurice et al., 1996). Although work should continue related to the development of new curricula, attention to the technology of fluency must also be examined. As a recent development in the field of autism, the concept of fluency holds promise as an emerging technology (Weiss, 2001).

LEARNING OUTCOMES ASSOCIATED WITH BEHAVIORAL FLUENCY

As students progress through levels of learning, educators should assess whether the skills attained are functional and learned to a level where they can be used in everyday life. Three learning outcomes are associated with behavioral fluency: retention, endurance, and application. Frequency ranges called performance standards predict these outcomes.

Retention

Retention is the ability to retain information after a period of time during which a person has not had an opportunity for practice (Binder, 1996). Results from behavioral fluency research shows that as students become more accurate and/or attain fluency, they show high degrees of retention (Berens, Boyce, Berens, Doney, & Kenzer, 2003; Brown, Dunne, & Cooper, 1996; Bucklin, Dickinson, & Brethower, 2000; Ivarie, 1986; Peladeau, Forget, & Gagne, 2003; Shimamune & Jitsumori, 1999). Figure 1 shows a visual representation of retention for a hypothetical student. In Figure 1, each tick mark on the line stands for 1 day. The first X on the first tick mark indicates that the student has met his goal and has stopped practicing a target skill. The next X, measured 47 days later, demonstrates how well the student has retained the skill. In this example, the student was asked to state the names and corresponding symbols from the periodic table of elements. The student learned the 29 transition metals (e.g., Cadmium—Cd, Nickel—Ni, Silver—Ag); 47 days later the teacher measured how well the student remembered the symbols for the names. If the student reached fluency, he would retain most if not all of the information. If the student did not reach fluency, the 47-day measure would reveal how much the student had retained. To gain fluency, the student must have both accuracy and speed, and, if desired, the student must practice naming the symbols with the names quickly and accurately.

Endurance

Endurance has characteristics similar to athletic stamina. For instance, a runner who has endurance runs at an even pace for a given distance (e.g., 400 m) and does not fatigue. When a student has endurance, he can perform at a steady pace for a given time (Binder, 1996) and is less resistant to distraction (Binder, Haughton, & Van Eyk, 1990). Research suggests students can overcome endurance problems as a result of increasing behavioral fluency (Berens et al., 2003; Binder et al., 1990; Haughton, 1980; Kim, Carr, Templeton, & Bird, 2001; McDowell & Keenan, 2001).

Figure 2 shows two profiles displaying the presence and absence of endurance. In the top line of the figure, each tick mark depicts 1 sec of time and the presence of a response. As shown in Figure 2, each response occurs one after the other in a rhythmic manner. The bottom of the figure shows a response that varies, appears disjointed, and does not proceed in an even manner. Binder et al. (1990) reported research showing the effects of endurance on numeral writing. Students practiced writing at varying time intervals on different days. The intervals ranges were 15 sec, 30 sec, 1 min, 2 min, 4 min, 8 min, and 16 min. Results indicated that students who wrote at a rate of 70 digits per minute showed a

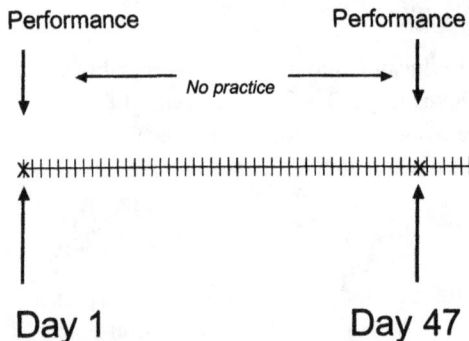

FIGURE 1   A visual example showing retention.

*Graphic display of responses in a
30-second interval of time*

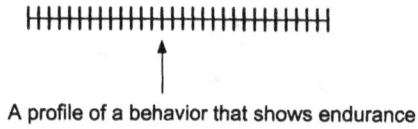

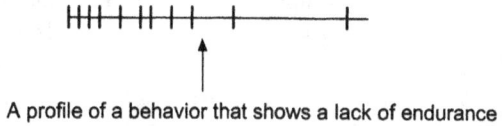

A profile of a behavior that shows endurance

FIGURE 2   Two profiles showing
the presence and absence of endurance.

A profile of a behavior that shows a lack of endurance

similar performance across the timing intervals. Students who wrote fewer than 70 digits had problems when they attempted to write numerals for longer periods of time. Results from the study illustrated that fatigue, or lack of endurance, prohibited some students from successfully engaging in the writing task.

Application

Application refers to a relationship between component behaviors and a compound behavior. Figure 3 graphically illustrates how two component skills can affect a compound or composite skill. An example of a component skill is handwriting. A composite skill is the integration of multiple component skills such as writing an essay. One of the component skills involved in essay writing is handwriting. Fluent component skills have an effect on a composite skill (Barrett, 1979; Binder, 1996; Haughton, 1972, 1980). When the

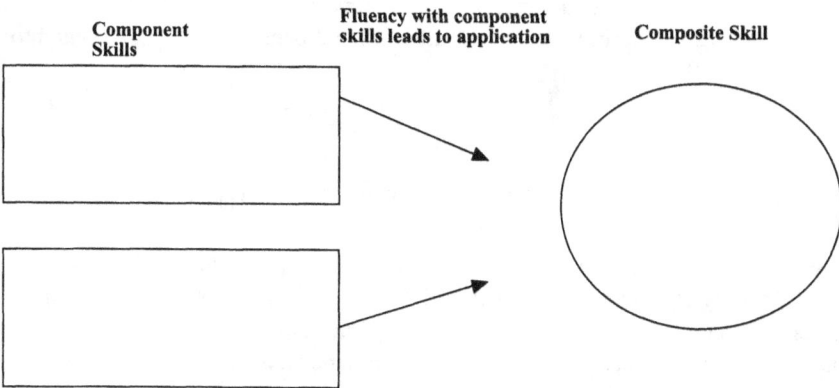

FIGURE 3   A model showing how two element or component skills can affect a compound or composite skill.

components reach fluency, teaching the composite occurs with greater facility (Binder, 1996; Haughton, 1980; Lin & Kubina, 2004). Behavioral fluency studies demonstrate support for the effective application of the components–composite relationship (Berens et al., 2003; Bucklin et al., 2000; Kubina, Young, & Kilwein, 2004; Lin & Kubina, 2004; McDowell & Keenan, 2002; McDowell, Keenan, & Kerr, 2002; McDowell, McIntyre, Bones, & Keenan, 2002; Smyth & Keenan, 2002).

Kubina et al. (2004) conducted a study showing how fluency with component behaviors helped students learn a composite behavior. The three students in the study were second-grade students with specific learning disabilities in reading. The students struggled to spell simple regular words like *mad, run,* and *he*. The intervention focused on building fluency with two component skills of the composite behavior. The component skills included hearing letter sounds and writing the corresponding letter (e.g., hear /h/ and write *h*) and segmenting words into their constituent sounds (e.g., hearing /had/ and saying each phoneme separately /h/ /a/ /d/) or developing phonemic awareness. As the participants became fluent with the two component skills, all three students performed the composite skill spelling regular words with 100% accuracy. The intervention never directly taught students how to spell words but instead only built fluency with the component skills.

Performance Standards

To achieve retention, endurance, and application, teachers and researchers use performance standards or fluency aims. Performance standards have a range of frequencies indicating a low and high end for fluency. Examples of performance standards for fluency include oral reading (i.e., 180 to 200 words per minute), writing answers to basic math facts (i.e., 70 to 90 digits per minute), and writing connected alphabet letters (i.e., 150+ words per minute; Beck & Clement, 1991; G. Freeman & Haughton, 1993a, 1993b). Performance standards serve as a numerical benchmark that predicts the occurrence of retention, endurance, and application (Johnson & Street, 2004). Haughton used the acronym REAPS (i.e., retention, endurance, application, performance standards) to describe the relationship between critical learning outcomes and behavioral fluency (Haughton, 1980; Lindsley, 1995).

BEHAVIORAL FLUENCY FOR STUDENTS WITH AUTISM

Although there is substantial empirical evidence for the use of behavioral fluency, a focused line of study demonstrating fluency and the critical learning outcomes for children with autism does not exist. However, incorporating fluency into the curriculum and other programmatic interventions holds great promise. Fluency may help students learn more and at a higher level. The following section provides examples of potential applications of behavioral fluency for students with autism.

Retention

Many curricula for students with autism focus on accuracy in skill attainment. For example, Taylor and McDonough (1993) broke the curriculum down into beginning, intermediate, and advanced skills. In a section entitled "Pre-academic Skills," the authors listed various matching skills such as matching pictures to identical pictures. With teacher instruction, a student could acquire the skill at a specified level of accuracy (e.g., 90%). However, accuracy will not necessarily result in long-term retainment of the skill.

Fluency, or accuracy plus speed, would require the student with autism to match the pictures very accurately and very quickly. Desired outcomes include that the student not only remembers the skill for long periods of time after instruction has ended but also performs the task with the regnant requirements in the environment. Further, students with behavioral fluency will also have opportunities to participate in activities and, thus, receive positive reinforcement. For example, during group instruction when the teacher holds up a yellow duck and asks, "What color is this duck?" the student who knows the answer will raise his or her hand and have the possibility of being called on and then receive verbal praise from the teacher for providing a correct answer. A student that needs 3 to 5 sec to identify a color will likely not have an opportunity to engage in the reinforcement contingency of providing an answer during group instruction. The potential research applications of fluency and retention extend to any skill and any desired time interval. As shown in Figure 1, an experimenter can insert a different skill and select any time interval and study the long-term retention effects associated with behavioral fluency.

Endurance

Simpson and Zionts (2000) noted that when students with autism become adults, they have a range of employment options open to them. To function in a workplace, a host of skills must reach the fluency level. Take the example of setting silverware in a restaurant. If a person is not fluent, then she or he will also lack endurance. As Figure 2 illustrates, if a person were to set silverware and lack endurance, her or his performance would be characterized by unsteady performance and susceptibility to distraction. Challenging behavior may be attributed to poor endurance. Binder et al. (1990) noted that students lacking endurance also may abandon a task or engage in escape behaviors due to the demands of the task. A lack of endurance could translate into so-called attention problems. Other examinations of endurance may indicate that the students stop or try to escape a skill not because they are uninterested in it but because a lack of endurance precludes the ability to successful engage in the behavior.

Application

As with almost any advanced skill, a number of component behaviors must be fluent. S. Freeman and Dake (1997) described a procedure to help students with autism learn whether they have enough money to purchase an item. The skills involved in the exercise include using a structured sheet to record an item, the price of an item, and the amount of money the student has. If the person has enough money he or she can purchase the item. Some of the component skills necessary to make the exercise work effectively are handwriting, adding, and subtracting. If the student is slow in any of the components, the composite behavior of determining "Do I have enough money?" will be affected. The critical learning outcome of application is more than task analyzing a composite behavior and analyzing if a student can do it accurately. Behavioral fluency enhances the functionality of the skill.

Any composite skill may be subjected to an experimental investigation of application. Composite behaviors that contain two of more components have an effect on terminal behavior. How fast and accurately a student can perform the component behaviors directly relates to how fast the student can execute the composite behavior. Deficiencies in social skills are very common in students with autism (Volkmar, Carter, Grossman, & Klin, 1997). However, competent use of social skills requires a number of components including recognition of social cues, nonverbal behaviors, the reception and integration of social feedback, and the ability to discriminate social situations (Hazel, Schumaker, Sherman, & Sheldon-Wildgen, 1983). The difference between being accurate but slow versus fluent with a component skill may help advance the understanding and practice of social skill performance.

Performance Standards

Performance standard research could take the form of individually or jointly testing the effects of retention, endurance, and application. For instance, matching objects to identical objects may provide long-term retention, endurance, and application when a student can correctly match objects at a frequency of 10 objects per 10 sec, or 60 objects per minute. Because fluency involves accuracy and time, the resulting performance standards offer a standard measure all students can be compared with—frequency.

Although performance standards for some academic behaviors for students without autism exist (e.g., Beck, Conrad, & Anderson, 1996; Mercer, Mercer, & Evans, 1982), researchers can employ several methods to find performance standards for students with autism. Some of the methods include (a) data gathered from special projects and research, (b) peer fluency data, (c) adult–child proportional formula, and (d) adult fluency data (Binder, 1996; Koorland, Keel, & Ueberhorst, 1990).

CONCLUSION

The research database for behavioral fluency clearly shows positive and substantial effects of behavioral fluency for students with and without disabilities. Although effects have not yet been systematically extended to students with autism, fluency has the potential to produce the critical learning outcomes of long-term retention, endurance, and application for all students with autism. Certainly due caution is always warranted with new lines of research and subsequent practical applications; however, it appears that behavioral fluency has the potential to bring us a step closer to providing maximal learning for students with autism.

REFERENCES

Alberto, P. A., & Troutman, A. C. (2003). *Applied behavior analysis for teachers* (6th ed.). Upper Saddle, NJ: Merrill.

Barrett, B. (1979). Communitization and the measured message of normal behavior. In R. York & E. Edgar (Eds.), *Teaching the severely handicapped* (Vol. 4, pp. 301–318). Columbus, OH: Special Press.

Beck, R., & Clement, R. (1991). The Great Falls Precision Teaching Project: An historical examination. *Journal of Precision Teaching, 8*(2), 8–12.

Beck, R., Conrad, D., & Anderson, P. (1996). *Basic skill builders handbook.* Longmont, CO: Sopris West.

Berens, K., Boyce, T. E., Berens, N. M., Doney, J. K., & Kenzer, A. L. (2003). A technology for evaluation relations between response frequency and academic performance outcomes. *Journal of Precision Teaching and Celeration, 19*(1), 20–34.

Binder, C. (1996). Behavioral fluency: Evolution of a new paradigm. *The Behavior Analyst, 19,* 163–197.

Binder, C., Haughton, E., & Van Eyk, D. (1990). Increasing endurance by building fluency: Precision teaching attention span. *Teaching Exceptional Children, 22*(3), 24–27.

Brown, S. A., Dunne, J. D., & Cooper, J. O. (1996). Immediate retelling's effect on student retention. *Education and Treatment of Children, 19,* 387–407.

Bucklin, B. R., Dickinson, A. M., & Brethower, D. M. (2000). A comparison of the effects of fluency training and accuracy training on application and retention. *Performance Improvement Quarterly, 13,* 141–163.

Dunlap, G. (1984). The influence of task variation and maintenance tasks on the learning and affect of autistic children. *Journal of Experimental Psychology, 37,* 41–64.

Engelmann, S. (1997). Direct instruction. In C. R. Dills & A. J. Romiszowski (Eds.), *Instructional development paradigms* (pp. 371–389). Englewood Cliffs, NJ: Educational Technology Publications.

Freeman, G., & Haughton, E. (1993a). Building reading fluency across the curriculum. *Journal of Precision Teaching, 10*(2), 29–30.

Freeman, G., & Haughton, E. (1993b). Handwriting fluency. *Journal of Precision Teaching, 10*(2), 31–32.

Freeman, S., & Dake, L. (1997). *Teach me language: A language manual for children with autism, Asperger's syndrome and related developmental disorders.* Langley, British Columbia, Canada: SKF Books.

Frost, L. A., & Bondy, A. S. (1994). *The picture exchange communication system training manual.* Cherry Hill, NJ: Pyramid Educational Consultants.

Haughton, E. C. (1972). Aims: Growing and sharing. In J. B. Jordan & L. S. Robbins (Eds.), *Let's try doing something else kind of thing* (pp. 20–39). Arlington, VA: Council for Exceptional Children.

Haughton, E. C. (1980). Practicing practices: Learning by activity. *Journal of Precision Teaching, 1*(3), 3–20.

Hazel, J. S., Schumaker, J. B., Sherman, J. A., & Sheldon-Wildgen, J. S. (1983). Social skills training with court-adjudicated youths. In C. LeCroy (Ed.), *Social skills training for children and youth* (pp. 117–137). New York: Haworth.

Howell, K. W., & Lorson-Howell, K. A. (1990). What's the hurry: Fluency in the classroom. *Teaching Exceptional Children, 22*(3), 20–27.

Ivarie, J. J. (1986). Effects of proficiency rates on later performance of a recall and writing behavior. *RASE: Remedial and Special Education, 7*(5), 25–30.

Johnson, K., & Layng, T. V. J. (1992). Breaking the structuralist barrier: Literacy and numeracy with fluency. *American Psychologist, 47,* 1475–1490.

Johnson, K., & Street, E. M. (2004). *The Morningside model of generative instruction: What it means to leave no child behind.* Concord, MA: Cambridge Center for Behavioral Studies.

Kim, C., Carr, J. E., Templeton, A., & Bird, S. (2001). Effects of fluency building on performance over "long" durations and in the presence of a distracting social stimulus. *Journal of Precision Teaching and Celeration, 17*(2), 7–26.

Koorland, M. A., Keel, M. C., & Ueberhorst, P. (1990). Setting aims for precision learning. *Teaching Exceptional Children, 22*(3), 64–66.

Kubina, R. M., & Morrison, R. (2000). Fluency in education. *Behavior and Social Issues, 10,* 83–99.

Kubina, R. M., Young, A. E., & Kilwein, M. (2004). Examining an effect of fluency: Application of oral word segmentation and letters sounds for spelling. *Learning Disabilities: A Multidisciplinary Journal, 13,* 17–23.

Leaf, R., & McEachin, J. J. (1998). *A work in progress: Behavior management strategies and a curriculum for intensive behavioral treatment of autism.* New York: Different Roads to Learning.

Lin, F. Y., & Kubina, R. M. (2004). Learning channels. *The Behavior Analyst Today, 5,* 1–14. Retrieved December 16, 2004, from http://www.behavior-analyst-online.org

Lindsley, O. R. (1995). Ten products of fluency. *Journal of Precision Teaching and Celeration, 13*(1), 2–11.

Lovaas, O. I. (2003). *Teaching individuals with developmental delays: Basic intervention techniques.* Austin, TX: Pro-Ed.

Maloney, M. (1998). *Teach your children well: A solution to some of North America's educational problems.* Cambridge, MA: Cambridge Center for Behavioral Studies.

Maurice, C., Green, G., & Luce, S. C. (1996). *Behavioral interventions for young children with autism: A manual for parents and professionals.* Austin, TX: Pro-Ed.

Mercer, C. D., & Mercer, A. R. (2001). *Teaching students with learning problems* (6th ed.). Upper Saddle River, NJ: Prentice Hall/Merrill.

Mercer, C. D., Mercer, A. R., & Evans, S. (1982). The use of frequency in establishing instructional aims. *Journal of Precision Teaching, 3*(3), 57–63.

McDowell, C., & Keenan, M. (2001). Developing fluency and endurance in a child diagnosed with attention deficit hyperactivity disorder. *Journal of Applied Behavior Analysis, 34,* 345–348.

McDowell, C., & Keenan, M. (2002). Comparison of two teaching structures examining the effects of component fluency on the performance of related skills. *Journal of Precision Teaching and Celeration, 18*(2), 16–29.

McDowell, C., Keenan, M., & Kerr, K. P. (2002). Comparing levels of dysfluency among students with mild learning difficulties and typical students. *Journal of Precision Teaching and Celeration, 18*(2), 37–48.

McDowell, C., McIntyre, C., Bones, R., & Keenan, M. (2002). Teaching component skills to improve golf swing. *Journal of Precision Teaching and Celeration, 18*(2), 61–66.

Peladeau, N., Forget, J., & Gagne, F. (2003). Effect of paced and unpaced practice on skill application and retention: How much is enough? *American Educational Research Journal, 40,* 769–801.

Scheuermann, B., & Webber, J. (2002). *Autism: Teaching does make a difference.* Belmont, CA: Wadsworth.

Shimamune, S., & Jitsumori, M. (1999). Effects of grammar instruction and fluency training on the learning of the and a by native speakers of Japanese. *Analysis of Verbal Behavior, 16,* 3–16.

Simpson, R. L., & Zionts, P. (2000). *Autism: Information and resources for professionals and parents* (2nd ed.). Austin, TX: Pro-Ed.

Smyth, P., & Keenan, M. (2002). Compound performance: The role of free and controlled operant components. *Journal of Precision Teaching and Celeration, 18*(2), 3–15.

Sundberg, M. L., & Partington, J. W. (1998). *Teaching language to children with autism or other developmental disabilities.* Pleasant Hill, CA: Behavior Analysts.

Taylor, B. A., & McDonough, K. A. (1993). Selecting teaching programs. In C. Maurice, G. Green, & S. C. Luce (Eds.), *Behavioral intervention for young children with autism: A manual for parents and professionals* (pp. 63–177). Austin, TX: Pro-Ed.

Volkmar, F., Carter, A., Grossman, J., & Klin, A. (1997). Social development in autism. In D. J. Cohen & F. R. Volkmar (Eds.), *Handbook of autism and pervasive developmental disorders* (2nd ed., pp. 171–194). New York: Wiley.

Weiss, M. J. (2001). Expanding ABA intervention in intensive programs for children with autism: The inclusion of natural environment training and fluency based instruction. *The Behavior Analyst Today, 2,* 182–185. Retrieved November 20, 2004, from http://www.behavior-analyst-online.org

Wolery, M., Jones-Ault, M., & Munson-Doyle, P. (1992). *Teaching students with moderate to severe disabilities.* White Plains, NY: Longman.

EXCEPTIONALITY, *13*(1), 45–53

Treatment of Multiply Controlled Problem Behavior With Procedural Variations of Differential Reinforcement

Pamela L. Neidert, Brian A. Iwata, and Claudia L. Dozier

Department of Psychology
University of Florida

We describe the assessment and treatment of 2 children with autism spectrum disorder whose problem behaviors (self-injury, aggression, and disruption) were multiply controlled. Results of functional analyses indicated that the children's problem behaviors were maintained by both positive reinforcement (attention) and negative reinforcement (escape from task demands). Subsequently, procedural variations of differential reinforcement and extinction were implemented in different contexts (attention and demand) and were effective in reducing problem behavior, increasing appropriate communication, and increasing compliance.

Although impairments in social interaction and communication are the primary behavioral characteristics of autism, problem behaviors such as stereotypy and self-injurious behavior (SIB) are also commonly seen (American Psychiatric Association, 1994). In a review of behavioral interventions for children with autism (8 years of age or younger), Horner, Carr, Strain, Todd, and Reed (2002) reported that stereotypy, aggression, SIB, property destruction, and tantrums were the problem behaviors most frequently referred for treatment. These behaviors present a challenge to parents and teachers of children with autism because improvement is unlikely to occur without formal intervention.

Treatment procedures that are effective in decreasing problem behavior while increasing communicative and social behavior are particularly desirable for children with autism. One such class of interventions is differential reinforcement of alternative behavior (DRA); in one variation of DRA, problem behavior is replaced with some form of communicative response. Often described as functional communication training (FCT), the procedure involves teaching the individual a socially appropriate way to gain access to the reinforcer that currently maintains problem behavior (Carr & Durand, 1985). FCT is commonly combined with extinction (EXT), in which reinforcement for problem be-

---

Requests for reprints should be sent to Brian A. Iwata, Department of Psychology, University of Florida, 114 Psychology Building, P.O. Box 112250, Gainesville, FL 32611–2250. E-mail: iwata@ufl.edu

havior is discontinued. In fact, a number of studies have shown that EXT may be a critical component of FCT (Fisher et al., 1993; Kelly, Lerman, & Van Camp, 2002; Shirley, Iwata, Kahng, Mazaleski, & Lerman, 1997).

The successful implementation of both FCT and EXT requires identification of the source of reinforcement for problem behavior, and functional analysis methodology (see Iwata, Kahng, Wallace, & Lindberg, 2000, for a review) has become the assessment tool of choice because it provides a basis for developing intervention procedures that match the functional characteristics of behavior. For example, teaching a child to request attention from the teacher (positive reinforcement) would not be expected to reduce problem behavior that is maintained by escape from task demands (negative reinforcement). Similarly, withholding attention may extinguish problem behavior maintained by attention but would have little effect on problem behavior maintained by escape. Thus, results of a functional analysis determine which procedural variations of FCT and EXT should be used in a particular case.

Several reports have indicated that problem behaviors occasionally may be maintained by more than one source of reinforcement (Day, Horner, & O'Neill, 1994; Smith, Iwata, Vollmer, & Zarcone, 1993). For example, because both aggression and SIB so often produce a variety of social consequences, individuals who acquire these behaviors because they produce attention may learn that the behaviors also are effective means of escape, and vice versa. When the same behavior serves multiple functions, each function must be addressed, usually in a different context and with a different treatment. FCT is an attractive option for treating problem behavior having multiple social functions because its procedural variations share common features even though the form of the response being taught and its associated reinforcer differ (e.g., "Play with me" followed by attention vs. "Done" followed by a break from an ongoing task). Results of several studies have indicated that FCT may be an effective treatment for multiply controlled problem behavior (Braithwaite & Richdale, 2000; Day et al., 1994; Hagopian, Wilson, & Wilder, 2001), and the purpose of this study was to evaluate the effectiveness of FCT + EXT both to reduce multiply controlled problem behavior and to increase the communicative skills of two young children with autism spectrum disorders.

METHOD

Participants and Setting

Two children seen in an outpatient clinic specializing in the assessment and treatment of severe problem behavior participated. Alison was a 3-year-old girl diagnosed with Pervasive Developmental Disorder Not Otherwise Specified, whose problem behaviors consisted of SIB, aggression, and disruption. Peter was a 4½-year-old boy diagnosed with autism whose problem behaviors consisted of SIB and aggression. Both children had limited verbal repertoires but were able to use one- to two-word phrases and simple gestures and could follow single-step instructions.

Sessions were conducted in clinic therapy rooms equipped with one-way observation windows. Rooms were equipped with a table, several chairs, and materials relevant to the specific conditions. Two- to 4-hr clinic appointments were conducted weekly for either 6 months (Alison) or 3 months (Peter). Sessions during each weekly appointment lasted 10 min.

Response Measurement and Reliability

Trained graduate and undergraduate students collected data on the frequency of SIB (head banging, self-biting, self-hitting, or self-scratching), aggression (hitting, kicking, biting, scratching, head butting others, or throwing objects at others), and disruption (property destruction, throwing objects, or knocking over furniture). Data also were collected on the frequency of prompted and unprompted communicative responses (card exchanges by Alison; vocal requests by Peter) during treatment. Frequency data were converted to number of responses per minute for purposes of data analysis. Interobserver agreement was not assessed for Peter's data due to our inability to schedule additional observers during his appointments. Interobserver agreement for Alison's problem and communicative behaviors was assessed during 19% of her sessions by having a second observer simultaneously but independently collect data with the primary observer. Sessions were divided into 10-sec intervals, and data were compared on an interval-by-interval basis. Agreement coefficients were calculated by dividing the smaller number of responses in each interval by the larger number of responses; these fractions were averaged across intervals and multiplied by 100%. Mean agreement scores for problem and communicative behaviors were 98% and 97%, respectively.

Functional Analysis

A functional analysis (Iwata, Dorsey, Slifer, Bauman, & Richman, 1982/1994) was conducted for each child to identify the consequences that maintained problem behavior. The assessment consisted of four conditions arranged in a multielement design. During the attention condition, the child and a therapist were in a room. The therapist asked the child to play independently with toys, then ignored the child except to deliver attention following occurrences of problem behavior. The purpose of the attention condition was to determine if problem behavior was maintained by positive reinforcement (access to attention). During the demand condition, a therapist presented academic (e.g., imitation, color identification, etc.) and hygienic (e.g., brush hair, wipe table, etc.) tasks to the child using a three-step prompting sequence (verbal, gestural, physical prompts). Compliance produced verbal praise; problem behavior produced a brief break (30 sec) from the task. The purpose of the demand condition was to determine if problem behavior was maintained by negative reinforcement (escape from demands). During the ignore condition, the child and a therapist were in a room; however, the therapist never interacted with the child. The purpose of the ignore condition was to determine if problem behavior was maintained by automatic reinforcement (persisted in the absence of social contingencies). During the play condition, no task demands were presented, and preferred toys and attention were continuously available. No programmed consequences were arranged for problem behavior. The purpose of the play condition was to serve as the control condition, against which the test conditions were compared.

Results of the functional analysis showed that the problem behavior of both children was multiply controlled, maintained by both positive reinforcement (attention) and negative reinforcement (escape). Therefore, each child was taught two functional alternative responses during treatment in different contexts: One response produced attention, and the other response produced escape. A multiple baseline design across behavioral functions was used to evaluate the effectiveness of FCT + EXT on rates of problem and communicative behavior.

Treatment Conditions

Baseline.   Two baselines conditions were conducted with each child. One baseline was the same as the attention condition of the functional analysis; the other was the same as the demand condition of the functional analysis.

FCT (attention) + EXT.   This intervention was implemented during the attention condition. Problem behavior no longer produced attention (EXT). Instead, communicative responses produced approximately 20 sec of attention. Alison's response was to hand a picture card to the therapist (depicting a photo of Alison playing with an adult). Peter's response was to say, "Play with me." The therapist initially prompted the child to emit the communicative response and then delivered attention. Subsequently, a prompt-delay procedure was used to fade therapist prompting. Increasingly longer delays between the occurrence of a communicative response and subsequent prompts to communicate were inserted contingent upon the completion of sessions in which rates of problem behavior were low (approximately at or below 10% of baseline rates). The prompt-delay procedure continued until the child exclusively emitted unprompted communicative responses.

FCT (escape) + EXT.   This intervention was implemented during the demand condition. Problem behavior no longer produced escape from demands (EXT). Instead, communicative responses produced a 30-sec break from demands. Alison's response was to hand a card to the therapist (depicting a photo of a stop sign). Peter's response was to say, "Break please." The therapist initially prompted the child to request a break immediately following a prompt to complete a task, then gave the child a break. The prompt-delay procedure just described was used to fade prompts to communicate until the child emitted the communicative response independently. An additional, differential reinforcement component was subsequently added to treatment for Alison to increase compliance with demands. Specifically, Alison received a preferred edible contingent upon compliance with demands.

RESULTS

Figure 1 shows the results of Alison's and Peter's functional analysis. Both children exhibited higher rates of problem behavior in the attention and demand conditions relative

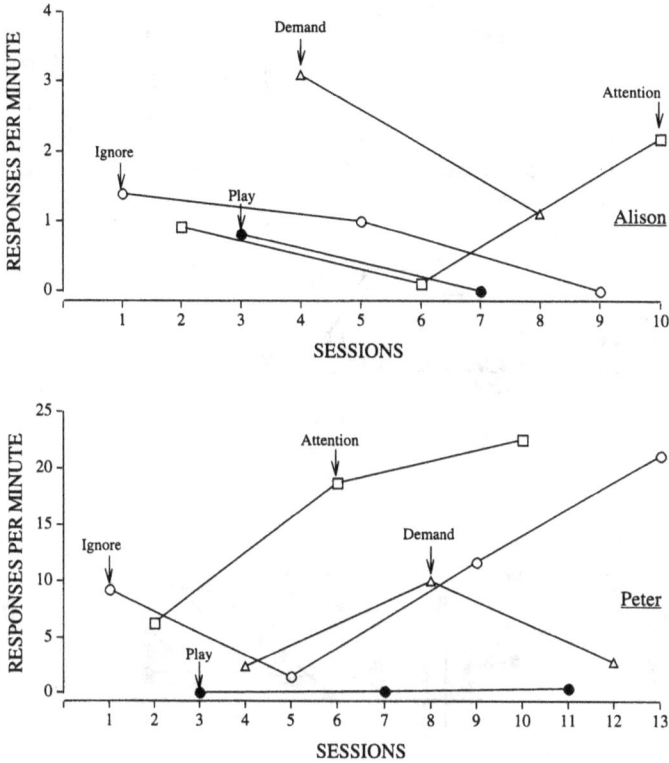

FIGURE 1   Rates of problem behavior exhibited by Alison and Peter during their functional analyses.

to the play (control) condition. This pattern of responding suggested that their problem behavior was maintained by both positive and negative reinforcement.

The top two panels of Figure 2 show Alison's treatment results. In the attention condition (upper panel), high rates of problem behavior were observed during baseline. FCT + EXT resulted in immediate and sustained decreases in problem behavior (with the exception of two sessions in which bursts of problem behavior occurred). Independent (unprompted) communication emerged and maintained occurred across sessions. Alison's extended admission to the outpatient clinic allowed additional session time to thin the reinforcement schedule for communication. A graduated multiple-schedule arrangement was used, in which signaled periods of reinforcement and extinction for communicative responses were alternated (see Hanley, Iwata, & Thompson, 2001, for details). The thinning procedure initially consisted of a 45-sec period during which all communicative responses were reinforced, followed by a 15-sec period during which reinforcement was unavailable. The terminal schedule was one in which a 1-min reinforcement period was followed by a 2-min EXT period. In the demand condition (lower panel), consistently high rates of problem behavior and low

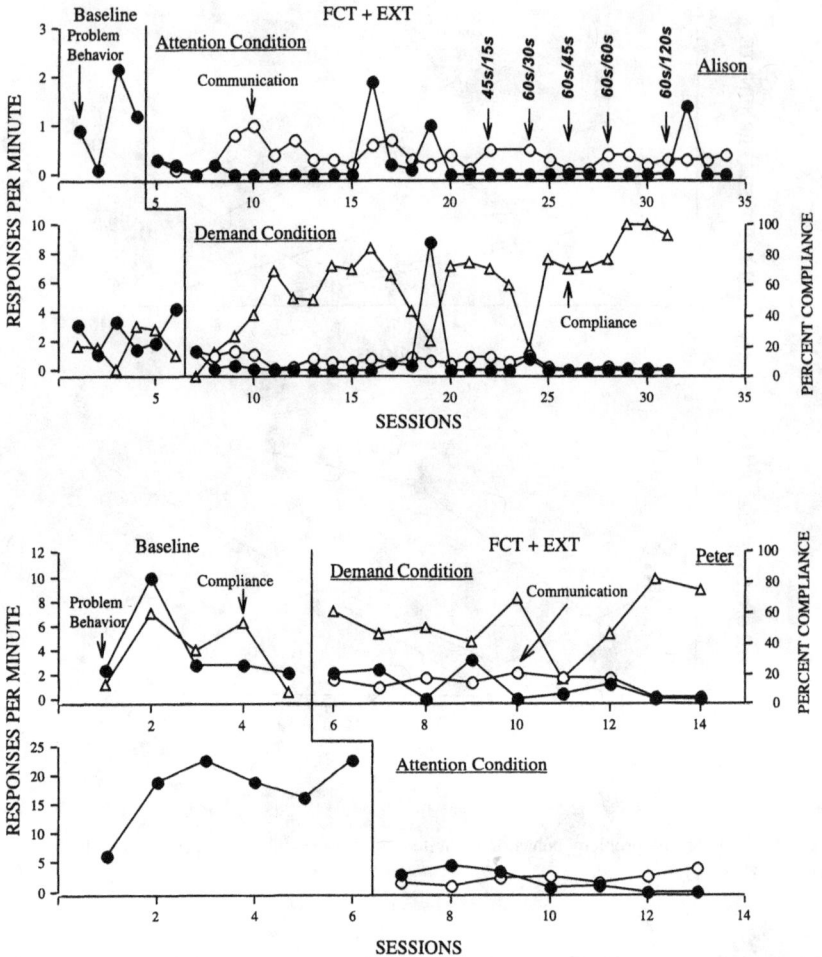

FIGURE 2   Treatment results for Alison and Peter. Alison's problem behavior and communicative behavior in the attention context are shown in the top panel; her problem behavior, communicative behavior, and compliance in the demand context are shown in the second panel. Peter's problem behavior, communicative behavior, and compliance in the demand context are shown in the third panel; his problem behavior and communicative behavior in the attention context are shown in the fourth panel. FCT = functional communication training; EXT = extinction.

levels of compliance were observed during baseline. FCT + EXT resulted in immediate and sustained decreases in problem behavior and consistent rates of independent communication. In addition, levels of compliance increased as compared to baseline levels with the addition of the differential reinforcement of compliance component.

The bottom two panels of Figure 2 show Peter's treatment results. In the demand condition (upper panel), high rates of problem behavior and low levels of compliance were observed during baseline. FCT + EXT resulted in a gradual decrease in problem behavior. Independent communication emerged during the first session and continued to occur consistently across sessions. In addition, Peter's compliance increased relative to baseline levels without the inclusion of additional interventions. In the attention condition (lower panel), extremely high rates of problem behavior were observed during baseline. FCT + EXT resulted in immediate and sustained decreases in problem behavior. Independent communication emerged during the first session and was maintained across sessions. Due to the short duration of Peter's clinic admission, reinforcement schedule thinning was not evaluated.

The parents of both children were trained to implement the treatment procedures initially during role-play sessions and subsequently during in vivo treatment sessions with their children. Both caregivers demonstrated a high degree of accuracy implementing treatment sessions. Parental reports following the completion of outpatient treatment indicated that both children continued to communicate for attention and escape from demands and engaged in little problem behavior both at home and at school. Alison's mother also reported that Alison began to *vocally* request (rather than exchanging picture cards) attention, breaks from demands, and various other preferred items and activities.

DISCUSSION

Results of this study illustrate the use of procedural variations of differential reinforcement as treatment for multiply controlled problem behavior. Results of functional analyses indicated that the two children's problem behaviors were maintained by both positive and negative reinforcement. Subsequently, FCT + EXT interventions for each function were implemented in different contexts and were associated with decreases in problem behavior, increases in appropriate communicative behavior, and increases in compliance.

The assessment results add to a growing body of literature indicating that the same problem behavior in the same individual may be maintained by different sources of reinforcement. In the case illustrated here, both children's assessment data suggested that a single intervention was unlikely to be very effective in managing their behavior across situational contexts. Although the data showed some variability, suggesting that assessment should have continued longer, the time constraints imposed by weekly outpatient appointments prevented lengthy assessment. Nevertheless, results for both children were relatively clear and are representative of outcomes obtained from brief functional analyses (Northup et al., 1991; Wacker et al., 1994; Wallace & Knights, 2003).

Two types of interventions were designed to address the multiple functions identified through assessment. One intervention (implemented in the attention context) involved teaching an alternative attention-seeking response while ignoring problem behavior; the other (implemented in the demand context) involved teaching an alternative escape response while not allowing problem behavior to produce escape from ongoing tasks. Although the interventions were procedurally different, they were derived from the same general approach to treatment in that they included both differential reinforcement and extinction components. These characteristics of the intervention process illustrate two important points: (a) Different types of treatment may be required for the same behavior depending on the source of reinforcement that maintains it, and (b) differential reinforcement procedures are very flexible in accommodating a wide range of variation.

A limitation of our research is that the necessity of varying interventions across contexts was not shown. For example, Carr and Durand (1985) showed that FCT appropriate for attention-maintained problem behavior had little effect on children whose problem behavior was maintained by escape. Given the limitations imposed by the setting in which this study was conducted, we deemed this strategy infeasible. Nevertheless, a stronger demonstration of the need to match treatment with function would have been provided by alternating both interventions in both contexts and showing that FCT + EXT for attention-maintained behavior was ineffective when applied to escape-maintained behavior and vice versa.

REFERENCES

American Psychiatric Association. (1994). *Diagnostic and statistical manual of mental disorders* (4th ed.). Washington, DC: Author.

Braithwaite, K. L., & Richdale, A. L. (2000). Functional communication training to replace challenging behavior across two behavioral outcomes. *Behavioral Interventions, 15,* 21–36.

Carr, E. G., & Durand, V. M. (1985). Reducing behavior problems through functional communication training. *Journal of Applied Behavior Analysis, 18,* 111–126.

Day, H. M., Horner, R. H., & O'Neill, R. E. (1994). Multiple functions of problem behaviors: Assessment and intervention. *Journal of Applied Behavior Analysis, 27,* 279–289.

Fisher, W., Piazza, C., Cataldo, M., Harrell, R., Jefferson, G., & Conner, R. (1993). Functional communication training with and without extinction and punishment. *Journal of Applied Behavior Analysis, 26,* 23–36.

Hagopian, L. P., Wilson, D. M., & Wilder, D. A. (2001). Assessment and treatment of problem behavior maintained by escape from attention and access to tangible items. *Journal of Applied Behavior Analysis, 34,* 229–232.

Hanley, G. P., Iwata, B. A., & Thompson, R. A. (2001). Reinforcement schedule thinning following treatment with functional communication training. *Journal of Applied Behavior Analysis, 34,* 17–38.

Horner, R. H., Carr, E. G., Strain, P. S., Todd, A. W., & Reed, H. K. (2002). Problem behavior interventions for young children with Autism: A research synthesis. *Journal of Autism and Developmental Disabilities, 32,* 423–446.

Iwata, B. A., Dorsey, M. F., Slifer, K. J., Bauman, K. E., & Richman, G. S. (1994). Toward a functional analysis of self-injury. *Journal of Applied Behavior Analysis, 27,* 197–209. (Reprinted from *Analysis and Intervention in Developmental Disabilities, 2,* 3–20, 1982)

Iwata, B. A., Kahng, S., Wallace, M. D., & Lindberg, J. S. (2000). The functional analysis model of behavioral assessment. In J. Austin & J. E. Carr (Eds.), *Handbook of applied behavior analysis* (pp. 61–89). Reno, NV: Context Press.

Kelly, M. E., Lerman, D. C., & Van Camp, C. M. (2002). The effects of competing reinforcement schedules on the acquisition of functional communication. *Journal of Applied Behavior Analysis, 35,* 59–63.

Northup, J., Wacher, D., Sasso, G., Steege, M., Cigrand, K., Cook, J., et al. (1991). A brief functional analysis of aggressive and alternative behavior in an outclinic setting. *Journal of Applied Behavior Analysis, 24,* 509–522.

Shirley, M. J., Iwata, B. A., Kahng, S., Mazaleski, J. L., & Lerman, D. C. (1997). Does functional communication training compete with ongoing contingencies of reinforcement? An analysis during response acquisition and maintenance. *Journal of Applied Behavior Analysis, 30,* 93–104.

Smith, R. G., Iwata, B. A., Vollmer, T. R., & Zarcone, J. R. (1993). Experimental analysis and treatment of multiply controlled self-injury. *Journal of Applied Behavior Analysis, 26,* 183–196.

Wacker, D., Berg, W., Cooper, L., Derby, K., Steege, M., Northup, J., et al. (1994). The impact of functional analysis methodology on outpatient clinic services. *Journal of Applied Behavior Analysis, 27,* 405–407.

Wallace, M. D., & Knights, D. J. (2003). An evaluation of a brief functional analysis format within a vocational setting. *Journal of Applied Behavior Analysis, 36,* 125–128.

EXCEPTIONALITY, *13*(1), 55–63

Competent Learner Model for Individuals With Autism/PDD

Vicci Tucci
Tucci Learning Solutions, Inc.
Watsonville, California

Dan Hursh
Department of Advanced Educational Studies
West Virginia University

Richard Laitinen
Tucci Learning Solutions, Inc.
Watsonville, California

Austin Lambe
Achievekids
Palo Alto, California

In this article we outline components of the Competent Learner Model (CLM). Based on principles of applied behavior analysis, the model provides empirically based assessment, instruction, and evaluation for students with developmental disabilities, including autism.

The Competent Learner Model (CLM; Tucci, 1986) was developed to address the needs of teachers, administrators, and paraprofessional staff to enhance delivery of "best practice" instructional programs and services for children and youth with pervasive developmental disabilities (PDD; Tucci, 2004). The model provides a means to effect systemic change using empirically based assessment, instructional, and evaluative strategies based on principles of applied behavior analysis (Tucci, Hursh, & Laitinen, 2004). Recent and ongoing research report the use and benefits of CLM (Hursh, Laitinen, & Tucci, 2004; Hursh, Tucci, Laitinen, Lovaas, & Morris, 2004).

Requests for reprints should be sent to Vicci Tucci, Tucci Learning Solutions, Inc., 6 Hangar Way, Suite A, Watsonville, CA 95076. E-mail: vtucci@tuccionline.com

CLM AND INDIVIDUALS WITH AUTISM

Applied behavior analysis interventions for the habilitation of children with autism typically have been designed to increase attention, play, social, self-help, academic, and language skills and to decrease stereotypic, annoying, injurious, disruptive, and destructive behaviors. Although the CLM addresses these same goals, the goals are met through design and implementation rather than a traditional "skills" training approach. The CLM takes an approach somewhat similar to that of Koegel et al. (1989) in which learners with autism are taught pivotal learning-to-learn competencies. Whereas Koegel et al. focused on the pivotal behaviors of motivation and responding to multiple cues, the CLM focuses on teaching learners to become competent observers, listeners, talkers, problem solvers, participators, readers, and writers. The benefit of this approach is that the instructional programming for naive learners, such as children with autism and related disorders, is explicitly designed to establish those repertoires that allow a learner to benefit from increasingly typical instructional procedures, presentations, groupings, and formats.

EDUCATIONAL CONSULTATION

Parents and teachers of children with special needs face many challenges caring for and working with their charges, not the least of which is a continual search for and implementation of the best practices available. Typically, their search leads them to an "expert" in the field. This person is available, on some limited basis, to provide input and advice through the standard expert/consultation model of service delivery. The contact with these individuals, although well intentioned, is often limited both in time and in scope.

Many of us (educators, parents, and teachers) attend seminars, go to conferences, and complete coursework to enhance our ability to serve the children better. The information presented at these events is often inspiring. Like the advice and prescriptions received at the time of the consultant contact, we tend to respond initially with a high degree of compliance to the recommendations made. We also recognize that, over time, our best intentions wane. We require frequent "booster sessions" to keep responding as consistently as we did in the beginning. As a result, with our current model, we frequently witness short-term gains followed by inconsistent and sometimes frustrating long-term outcomes.

Current practices are limited by the actual time that the consultant has contact with the implementers. This is a serious limitation, because the drift that occurs—that is, the difference between what was recommended and what is actually being implemented—tends to increase over time to the detriment of the service. Absent the "expert" from the vagaries of minute-to-minute, day-to-day treatment and care, parents and teachers are faced with ever-changing conditions and variations to the presenting issues. Without the ability to adjust and manage the changing environment, they typically encounter fewer successes. If not managed correctly, this pattern often either leads to the parents or educators burning out or fosters an overdependence on the consultant and his or her time. Neither of these scenarios provides for the durability of programs that is necessary when caring for children with special needs.

FIVE ISSUES RELATED TO SYSTEMS CHANGE

Changing practices in ongoing programs is a great challenge and requires multiple efforts. Because practices and materials are recommended does not, ipso facto, mean they will be adopted. Effective and sustained system change efforts have five common characteristics: (a) "ownership"; (b) embedded, ongoing training and support; (c) validated curriculum delivered via (d) validated instructional procedures; and (e) continual evaluation and program enhancement. The CLM addresses the issue of ownership through collaborative consultation. Embedded training and support are accomplished, respectively, through the model's Course of Study (staff training) and Coaching (staff support) components. Validated curriculum and instructional procedures are established through a specifically designed Curriculum component. Continual evaluation and enhancement are accomplished through Performance Assessment, Coaching, and Collaborative Consultation components.

THE CLM: FIVE SOLUTIONS THAT EXEMPLIFY
BEST PRACTICES

The CLM learning solutions support educators and parents in their efforts to arrange instructional conditions to develop seven Competent Learner Repertoires (CLRs): Observing, Listening, Talking, Reading, Writing, Problem Solving, and Participating. When the CLRs are developed along with skills at using various learning tools, they allow for subject matter mastery, producing an augmentative and exponential effect on the development of day-to-day functional actions.

The CLM purposefully incorporates best practice recommendations from the disciplines of applied behavior analysis (Cooper, Heron, & Heward, 1987; Skinner, 1968), direct instruction (Engelmann & Carnine, 1982; Kame'enui & Simmons, 1990), and precision teaching (Lindsley, 1992). These practices clearly indicate the importance of systematic staff training, evaluation, and support, as well as systematic learner assessment, instruction, and evaluation. The CLM provides five solutions that address effective and sustained systems change. Each of the five solutions is discussed next.

CLM Course of Study

The CLM Course of Study prepares educators and parents to be successful at arranging and rearranging the parts of instructional conditions so that the CLRs develop and undesirable repertoires are weakened. The Course of Study uses programmed instruction with video examples within a personalized system of instruction that assures educators' and parents' mastery of necessary competencies through performance checkouts by trained CLM Coaches. The Course of Study has been shown to be associated with educators' and parents' success at selecting and arranging and rearranging contingencies appropriate for learners' repertoire development (Hursh, Laitinen, et al., 2004). The scope and sequence of the first 15 units of the course are displayed in Figure 1, showing

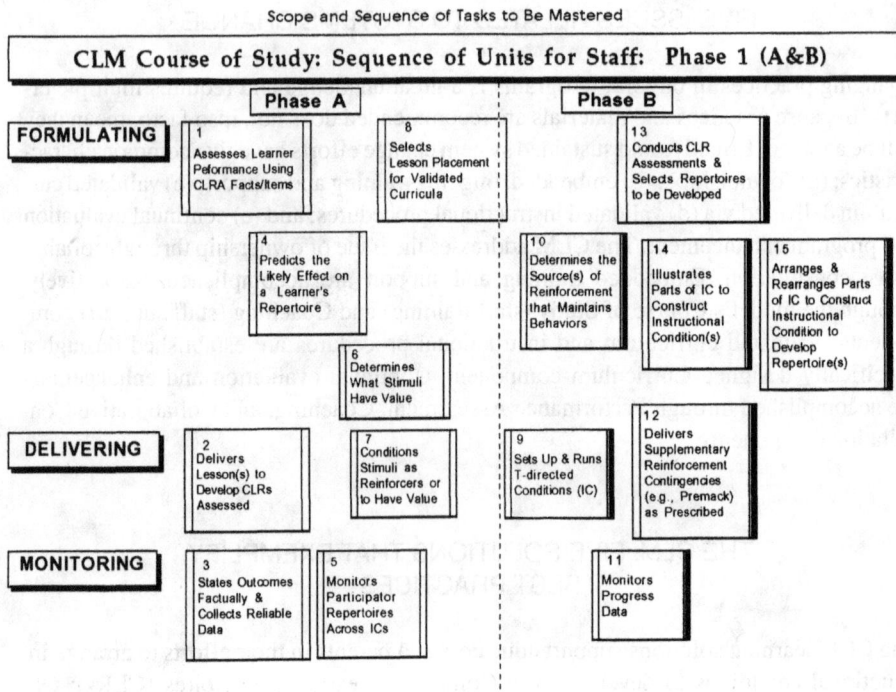

Scope and Sequence of Tasks to Be Mastered

CLM Course of Study: Sequence of Units for Staff: Phase 1 (A&B)

Phase A | **Phase B**

FORMULATING

1 Assesses Learner Peformance Using CLRA Facts/Items

8 Selects Lesson Placement for Validated Curricula

13 Conducts CLR Assessments & Selects Repertoires to be Developed

4 Predicts the Likely Effect on a Learner's Repertoire

10 Determines the Source(s) of Reinforcement that Maintains Behaviors

14 Illustrates Parts of IC to Construct Instructional Condition(s)

15 Arranges & Rearranges Parts of IC to Construct Instructional Condition to Develop Repertoire(s)

6 Determines What Stimuli Have Value

DELIVERING

2 Delivers Lesson(s) to Develop CLRs Assessed

7 Conditions Stimuli as Reinforcers or to Have Value

9 Sets Up & Runs T-directed Conditions (IC)

12 Delivers Supplementary Reinforcement Contingencies (e.g., Premack) as Prescribed

MONITORING

3 States Outcomes Factually & Collects Reliable Data

5 Monitors Participator Repertoires Across ICs

11 Monitors Progress Data

6/20/01   ©-2001-1997 Tucci Learning Solutions, Inc.

FIGURE 1   The scope and sequence of the units in the Competent Learner Model (CLM) Course of Study. CLRA = Competent Learner Repertoire Assessment; CLR = Competent Learner Repertoire; IC = Instructional Condition.

the way the units develop the formulating, delivering, and monitoring skills necessary for effective instruction.

CLM Coaching

The CLM Coaching is used to promote mastery of educators' and parents' CLM Course of Study units and for the eventual oversight of the arranging and rearranging of instructional conditions. Trained CLM Coaches are governed by the Personalized System of Instruction guidelines (e.g., Tutor as needed and Pace progress) as they monitor their educators' and parents' performance. They are brought to mastery of and fluency with the coaching competencies listed in the coaching checklist (see Figure 2).

CLM Curriculum

The CLM Curriculum has been developed to provide detailed instructional formats that are designed to systematically strengthen all seven CLRs (e.g., Talker and Participator). The curriculum consists of two levels that take the naive learner from CLRs that are not established to the establishment and maintenance of all seven CLRs across all appropri-

CLM Coaching Checklist: CLM Units 1-8

DIRECTIONS: Make a check mark (☐) in each of the boxes below where you observed the coach performing as expected. Leave the boxes blank where you did NOT observe the coach performing as expected. Place a hyphen mark (-) in the boxes if you **do not know** if something was performed as expected.

Established Collaborative Relationship

☐ Shared responsibility for participant's success or lack of as they complete the CLM Units

☐ Was very clear about who's in charge of learning environment

☐ Assisted participant in solving problems by making 'suggestions', if asked

Maintained 'Positive' Rapport

☐ Relied on 'user-friendly language' (jargon only when needed)

☐ Placed special emphasis on what the participant is doing that's 'right'

☐ If something is NOT occuring as expected, the coach 'suggested' what the participant can do to achieve success

☐ If possible, selected problems that are likely to be easy to solve

Provided 'Type of Coaching' Necessary to Function Independently

Tutored participant so s/he could perform successfully
  ☐ Assisted participant to apply what s/he has learned
  ☐ Prompted to lead to independent responding
  ☐ Attempted to FADE or faded the prompt(s) within session
  ☐ Reinforced the expected participant behaviors

Required a **remediation** session to assure for mastery
  ☐ **Required** participant to return to Unit to perform remediation session

Reinforce participants for applying what they are learning
  ☐ Scanned for opportunities to reinforce participants for applying what's being learned
  ☐ Arranged reinforcement contingency(s) to establish and maintain a consistent level of performance

Motivated the participant to apply what s/he has learned:
  ☐ Assisted an educator or parent to **identify** what they 'want' to 'get' their learner to do
  ☐ **Related** what the participants 'want' their learners to do to the tasks they are expected to perform.

Assessed participant abilities to decide what the coach can do:
  ☐ **Assessed** the participant abilities and **decided** what s/he can do to help participant to achieve a solution.
  ☐ Assisted participant to solve problem(s) **within the scope of Units 1-8**

Coach: _____ Participant: _____ Observer(s): _____ Unit: _____

Learne(s): _____ Setting: _____ Date: _____

revised 1/01/02   ©2002-2001 Tucci Learning Solutions, Inc

FIGURE 2   The Competent Learner Model (CLM) Coaching Checklist.

ate situations. The completion of the second level of the CLM Curriculum prepares many learners with autism/PDD to be successful in validated curricula at the kindergarten or beginning first-grade level of sophistication for normally developing children. Routine implementation of its instructional formats has been shown to be associated with the development of the student repertoires (CLRs; Hursh, Tucci, et al., 2004). Figure 3 displays the scope and sequence of the lessons for the Pre-1 Level of the CLM Curriculum and its articulation with Level 1.

CLM Performance Assessment and Performance Reviews

The CLM Performance Assessments (i.e., Competent Learner Repertoire Assessments [CLRAs] and Performance Reviews for Educators and Parents) assist educators and parents to appropriately place their learners in validated curricula by providing a profile of their learners' strengths and weaknesses across all seven CLRs. The CLRA has been shown to have concurrent validity with the Vineland Adaptive Behavior Scales, be sensitive to change in learner behavior, and have high interobserver agreement among educators using it to assess their learners (Deem, Hursh, & Tucci, 2004). The educators' and

CLM Curricula's Scope & Sequence:pre-1 & 1

LESSONS:	1	2	3	4	5	6	7	8	9	10	11	12	13	14	15	16

Participator
- 0.505 Selects, USES a variety of objects, & puts objects away in non-directed conditions within 2 minutes without annoying or injurious behaviors with T's help (1-16)
- 0.503 Completes one assigned task in semi-directed conditions w/T near; upto 20 parts/task (2-10)
- 1.503 Completes 2 consecutive (tasks @ 5 min/task) in s-d (11-22)
- 0.501 Performs 3 consecutive sets of 10 responses in t-d, 1:2 (3-14)
- 0.504 Accepts/Gives objects to peers w/T prompts (7-12)
- 1.504 Takes turns w/pref item w/in 1 min (13-33)
- 0.502 In Td, Answers on signal with FIRM items for 3 consec. sets of 10 (15-16)

Problem Solver
- 0.201 Spontaneously asks for preferred items or T actions using motor or vocl beh minimum of 12/hr. & waits @ 10 secs for item/action (1-9)
- 1.201 Spontaneously asks for missing item or T actions using phrases; waits 60 secs. (10-29)
- 0.801 Manipulates an object to place it or remove it from its location; @ 10 parts/problem (4-9)
- 0.203 Uses motor behavior to say "no" to an offer of a non-preferred item; tollerates 10 sec. delay of removing it (12-14)

Listener
- 0.601 Follows series of 5-7 FIRM single-step directions across variety of situations with T near, 1-5 feet away (3-12)
- 1.601 Performs series of 7-10 FIRM two-step directions. 5-10ft (13-29)
- 0.602 In display of 8, L touches pictures at a set fluency rate when pictures named (9-16)

Observer
- 0.701 Imitates the modeled single-step action performed by T (4-9)
- 1.701 Imitates the modeled two-step actions performed by Peers (10-33)
- 0.702 Finds ea. matching pix & places it below matching pix in 2-3 pix display (13-16)
- 0.102 Labels each picture in a field of 8-10 common items when T touches one (12-16)
- 0.703 Sorts 3 FIRM sets of similar pictures into separate piles and puts 1-2 distractors aside (4-13)

Talker
- 0.002 Repeats components of sounds or words related to preferred activities (3-8)
- 0.001 Repeats @ 20 common words w/out item displayed for preferred or non-pref nouns, verbs, attributes (8-14)

Reader
- 0.301 Repeats sounds or words when T is playfully reading a familiar story or T says, "Say, dog" (13-16)

Writer
- 0.401 Imitates direction or shape of the line once it is drawn by T on large paper w/markers... (4-12)
- 1.401 Copies 5-10 pre-drawn lines/shape on untimed paper... (12-29)

revised: 5/1/04   ©2004-1997 Tucci Learning Solutions, Inc.

FIGURE 3   The Competent Learner Model Levels Pre-1 and 1 Curriculum Scope and Sequence.

parents' performances are continually monitored to assess their ongoing performance in the CLM Course of Study and the delivery of what they have learned to do or say to develop their learners' competencies. Figure 4 displays the results of the CLRAs completed at entry and some months later for a learner whose parents and teachers were applying the CLM Curriculum and receiving Collaborative Consultation.

CLM Collaborative Consultation

The CLM Collaborative Consultation is the practice of providing assistance to educators and parents by making conspicuous the contingencies operating in a given situation. An ongoing functional analysis is conducted, which enables the behavior analyst to work

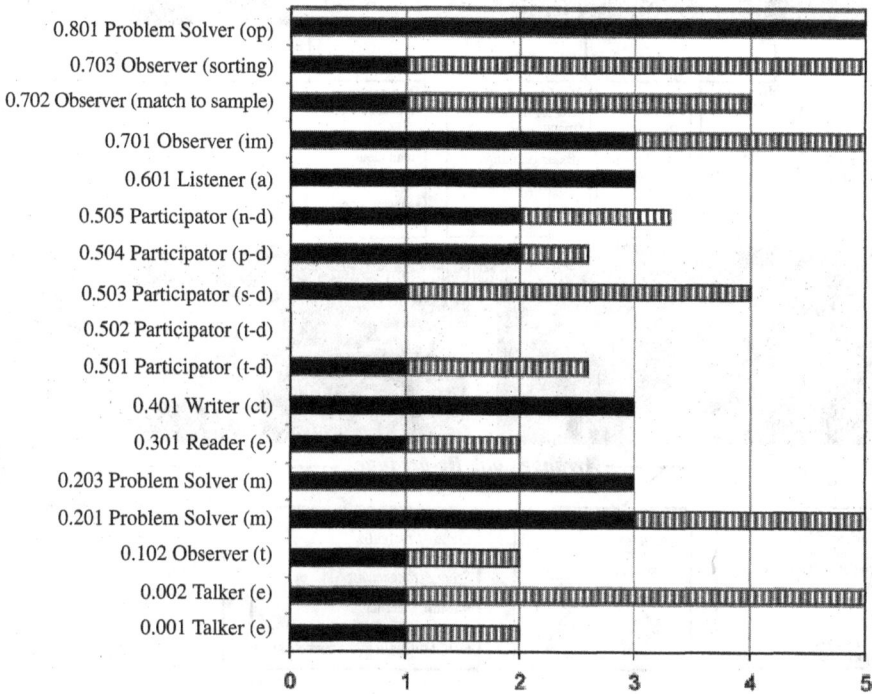

FIGURE 4   An example of results from the Competent Learner Repertoire Assessments. op = operate; im = imitate actions; a = adhere to advice; n-d = nondirected; p-d = peer-directed; s-d = semi-directed; t-d = teacher-directed; ct = copy text; e = echoic; m = mand; t = tact. Rating scale: 0 = no opportunity to observe; 1 = repertoire is not established; 2 = repertoire is established but response form is only approximated; 3 = repertoire is established but rarely performed across people, places, and items; 4 = repertoire is established but requires further development across people, places, and items; 5 = repertoire is mastered and performed consistently.

with the educator or parent to determine rearrangements of contingencies that might ensure the development of CLRs and the weakening of undesirable repertoires. These rearrangements are then tried, with further adjustments developed as needed. Throughout the consultation process, the behavior analyst recognizes that the real expertise in the situation lies with the educators and parents who live it every day. Figure 5 illustrates the relationship among the CLRs, Instructional Conditions available to develop the CLRs, and arranging and rearranging of the Parts of Instructional Conditions to assure the development of the CLRs.

CONCLUSION

In summary, the five learning solutions of the CLM illustrate best practices and how these best practices can be learned and applied. Parents and educators are provided with

Engineering Learning Environments: Overview

Develop
Competent Learner Repertoires©

Talker	Observer	Listener	Problem Solver	Reader	Writer	Participator
• repeat words (echoic) • answer wh-? (intraverbal)	• label (tact) • match to sample • imitate actions	• follow directions • abides by advice	• ask for things (mand) • fix or get things (operate)	• repeat sounds (echoic) • read aloud (textual) • answer questions (intraverbal)	• copy text • write word (takes dictation) • compose sentences (intraverbal))	• teacher-directed • semi-directed • peer-directed • non-directed

Construct
Instructional Conditions

Teacher-directed	Semi-directed	Peer-directed	Non-directed
• present lessons or set up for responding (i.e., Teacher sets occasion for each response & provides reinforcement for responses) • proximity at-hand	• present firm assignment (assignment sets occasion for responding & reinforces responding) • promixity near	• announce free-time or present an assignment (peers set occasion for responding & reinforce responding) • promixity near	• announce free-time or present an assignment (preferred activity or assignment sets occasion for responding & reinforces responding) • promixity near or far

Arrange and Re-arrange
Parts of Instructional Conditions

Curricula	Learners	Physical Structure	Teacher Delivery
• Sequence of Related Tasks • Validated Formats • Cumulative Reviews **Instructional Materials** • Lessons • Assignments • Preferred Activities • Project Kits	*Group learners* • same or • mixed level	*Choose Proximity:* • at-hand • near • far *Setup Arrangements* • u-shaped • cooperative • theatre • casual *Select Size* • 1:1 • sm. or lg group • whole class	• Set Up for Responding • Present Lessons (MLT) • Assign Tasks (e.g., SCR) • Announce Free-Choice

©1997, 1993 Tucci Educational Systems, Inc.

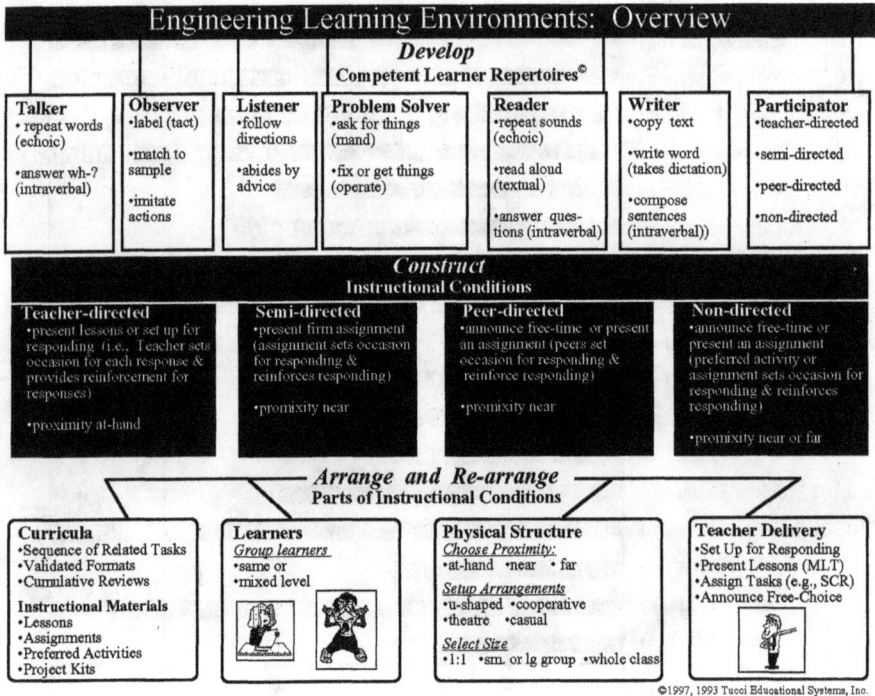

FIGURE 5   The engineering of learning environments for success using the Competent Learner Model. MLT = Model, Lead, and Test; SCR = Scan, Catch, and Reinforce.

competencies necessary to develop the CLRs of their children or students and to promote the learners' ability to function effectively in everyday circumstances.

REFERENCES

Cooper, J. O., Heron, T. E., & Heward, W. L. (1987). *Applied behavior analysis.* Englewood Cliffs, NJ: Prentice-Hall.

Deem, J., Hursh, D. E., & Tucci, V. (2004). *Inter-rater reliability and concurrent validity of the competent learner repertoire assessment.* Manuscript in preparation.

Engelmann, S., & Carnine, D. (1982). *Theory of instruction: Principles and application.* New York: Irvington.

Hursh, D. E., Laitinen, R. E., & Tucci, V. (2004, February). *An evaluation of the Competent Learner Model course of study.* Poster presented at the annual convention of the California Association for Behavior Analysis, San Francisco, CA.

Hursh, D. E., Tucci, V., Laitinen, R. E., Lovaas, C., & Morris, J. (2004, May). *The correlation between Program Implementation and Student Progress: Data from the Competent Learner Model.* Paper presented at the annual convention of the Association for Behavior Analysis, Boston.

Kame'enui, E. J., & Simmons, D. C. (1990). *Designing instructional strategies: The prevention of academic learning problems.* Columbus, OH: Merrill.

Koegel, R. L., Schreibman, L., Good, A., Cerniglia, L., Murphy, C., & Kern-Koegel, L. (1989). *How to teach pivotal behaviors to children with autism: A training manual.* (Available from the Department of Psychology, C–009, University of California, San Diego, La Jolla, CA 92093)

Lindsley, O. R. (1992). Precision teaching: Discoveries and effects. *Journal of Applied Behavior Analysis, 25,* 51–57.

Skinner, B. F. (1968). *The technology of teaching.* New York: Appleton-Century-Crofts.

Tucci, V. (1986, February). *An analysis of a competent learner.* Paper presented at the annual convention of the Northern California Association for Behavior Analysis, San Mateo, CA.

Tucci, V. (2004). *The Competent Learner Model: An introduction.* (Available from Tucci Learning Solutions, Inc., 6 Hangar Way, Suite A, Watsonville, CA 95076)

Tucci, V., Hursh, D. E., & Laitinen, R. E. (2004). The Competent Learner Model (CLM): A merging of Applied Behavior Analysis, Direct Instruction, and Precision Teaching. In D. J. Moran & R. Mallot (Eds.), *Evidence-based educational methods* (pp. 109–123). San Diego, CA: Elsevier.

For Product Safety Concerns and Information please contact our EU
representative GPSR@taylorandfrancis.com
Taylor & Francis Verlag GmbH, Kaufingerstraße 24, 80331 München, Germany